D1566298

The Politics of Small Things

**The Politics of Small Things: The Power of the
Powerless in Dark Times**

Jeffrey C. Goldfarb

The University of Chicago Press :: Chicago and London

38
44
47
59
89
94
104
151
132

Jeffrey C. Goldfarb is the Michael E. Gellert Professor of Sociology at the New School for Social Research. His books include *The Cynical Society* (1991) and *Beyond Glasnost* (1989), both published by the University of Chicago Press.

The University of Chicago Press, Chicago 60637
The University of Chicago Press, Ltd., London
© 2006 by The University of Chicago
All rights reserved. Published 2006
Printed in the United States of America

Portions of this book have been published elsewhere and are used here by permission of the publishers: parts of chapter 2 appeared in *The Blackwell Companion to the Sociology of Culture,* ed. Mark Jacobs and Nancy Weiss Hanrahan (Malden, MA: Blackwell, 2005); an earlier version of chapter 3 appeared as "1989 and the Creativity of the Political," *Social Research* 68, no. 4 (winter 2001): 993–1010; and a different version of chapter 5 appeared as "The Politics of Small Things," *The Communication Review* 8, no. 2 (April–June 2005): 159–83.

15 14 13 12 11 10 09 08 07 06   1 2 3 4 5

ISBN: 0-226-30108-7 (cloth)

Library of Congress Cataloging-in-Publication Data
Goldfarb, Jeffrey C.
    The politics of small things : the power of the powerless in dark times / Jeffrey C. Goldfarb.
        p.   cm.
    Includes bibliographical references and index.
    ISBN 0-226-30108-7 (cloth : alk. paper)
        1. Political sociology. 2. Social interaction—Political aspects.
    3. Politics and culture.   I. Title.
    JA76.G58 2006
    306.2—dc22
                                                        2005020976

♾ The paper used in this publication meets the minimum requirements of the American National Standard for Information Sciences—Permanence of Paper for Printed Library Materials, ANSI Z39.48-1992.

In memory of Michael Edward Asher
June 7, 1948–September 11, 2001

Contents

Acknowledgments

When I started my career, I wrote primarily for my teachers. I wanted to show them that I understood their lessons and could make something of them, that I could contribute. Then my attention shifted, and I primarily addressed my peers. Sometimes this was done in the spirit of competition, more often, I hope and think, in the spirit of collaboration. I tried, along with many different colleagues, in a number of different fields and from many different places, to develop critical social theory, thinking about new alternatives to modern tyranny, rethinking the promise of social movements and civil society, reflecting on the experience of the developing democratic movements in Eastern and Central Europe and their meaning for comparative inquiry. Teachers and colleagues are still on my mind and have continued to help me as I embarked on this project, the study of the politics of small things, and as I completed this book, the project's first phase, addressing the power of the powerless in dark times. I acknowledge for their lasting contribution to my foundational education Arnold Foster, Alicja Iwanska, Paul Meadows, Maurice Richter Jr., Howard S. Becker, Morris Janowitz, Donald Levine, Barry Schwartz, and Edward Shils. And I thank my colleagues who have particularly helped me in this endeavor through their writings and in conversations and criticisms, especially Talal Asad, Jose Casanova, Paolo Carpignano, Janos Kis, Xolela Mangcu,

Elzbieta Matynia, Adam Michnik, Robin Wagner Pacifici, Adriana Pa-
tryna, and Roger Shepherd.

Yet now, my primary focus has turned from my teachers and colleagues to my students. I try to present to them my understanding of the
world as they inherit it, both of the larger world of society, culture, and
politics and the more narrowly focused world of sociology and cultural
and political inquiry. They have in turn provided me with a way to continue my education, enabling me to draw on their perspectives and insights into the problems of our times. I am grateful for this.

At the New School, I teach in two distinct venues in New York, at the
Graduate Faculty of Political and Social Science in the sociology department, and at Eugene Lang College in the first-year program and in the social and historical inquiry concentration. I have worked with my graduate students in courses on the fundamental theories of the sociology of
culture and politics, the problems of social interaction, and the sociology
of media. The basic theoretical perspective presented in this book was
first formulated in these courses. I thank the students for their critical insights as they contributed to my ideas, and look forward to their development of their projects as they are informed by our shared explorations.
Many of them have already impressed me greatly with how far they can
go. At the College, I mostly teach first-year students. In our class meetings, I have been moved by their curiosity and intellectual growth. I find
this experience very rewarding. In these classes the power of the politics
of small things is revealed, as I explore in chapter 7.

Also in chapter 7, I consider what I have learned in special New
School Institutes on Democracy and Diversity in Krakow, Poland, and
Cape Town, South Africa. The students in these programs include advanced graduate students, young assistant professors, human rights activists, and other young leaders of democratic institutions and movements from Europe, Africa, Asia, and North and South America. Most
of these students are practitioners of the politics of small things as they
struggle for democratic ideals in less than ideal circumstances. I hope
they have learned as much from me and from each other in our seminar
meetings on democratic culture as I have learned from them. Although
these are dark times, it has been my good fortune to observe these sources
of light.

And a number of students have assisted me in researching and com-
posing this book. I thank Richard Cimino, Irit Dekel, Eran Fisher, and
Despina Lalaki for their help. While they have helped me in tracking down
sources and cleaning up citations, they more significantly have helped by
posing critical questions and comments. For assistance in the preparation

of the manuscript I also thank the secretary of the sociology department at the New School, Jaime Bradstreet.

This book was composed at a time of crisis. It was very much shaped by my attempt to confront this crisis, as I have witnessed it professionally and experienced it personally. I thank Naomi Gruson Goldfarb for being with me on this. Without her love, understanding, and support, I would not have been able to pull this off.

Introduction: In the Shadow of Big Things

In our daily lives, the forces of history are present. Economic conditions determine personal destiny. Political order shapes intimate relationships. Religious developments form individual character. But there is another side to this matter. Daily life shapes the economy, the polity, and civilization itself. In this inquiry, we will explore this side of things. We will explore how people make history in their social interactions. We will explore how democracy is in the details. This is ever more evident in the post–cold war era, as we learn more about what happened in the short, dark twentieth century, and as we realize the contours of our present political landscape with its new terrors.[1] Broad generalizations are the stuff of ideologists. Democrats must focus on finer stuff.

Modern thinking focused on two magical routes to the good and democratic society. Control the forces of production in a socialist fashion, and a democratic and just society would result. Free the market, and a democratic and free society would be achieved. Such totalized thinking about social and political problems was the ideological material of the cold war. But it was more than that. There was a general understanding that the power of the state and the power of the economy were the alternative means available to achieve the good society: state ownership or privatization, the plan or the invisible hand. For some the collapse of communism put an end to all this. Such people, including me, became convinced that the market and the state are modern instruments for practical action and have no meaning in and of themselves.[2] Others have maintained that the collapse of communism indicated the victory of capitalism: the victory of the economy over the state.[3] The inadequacy of radical privatization in much of the underdeveloping world, though, makes such a simple narrative unconvincing.[4]

As the great modern narratives lose their hold, as the grand march of the Western world loses its appeal,[5] people cannot figure out what to do. Injustices persist, and the simple solutions have been discredited. We see no alternatives, and this leads to despair, especially on the left but also on the right. This sense of hopelessness has been addressed feebly on the left: the "third way" tries to address social justice concerns, using market mechanisms, capitalism, as its instrument. In the United States, this approach led to the radical cuts in commitments to the poor associated with the Clinton administration. But hopelessness also leads to radical reaction formations. There are the actions of terrorists and antiterrorists, who imagine that their violent acts will right civilizational indignities and contemporary oppressions, and there is the rise of xenophobia, which imagines that all problems will be resolved if the other is not present, or is put in its proper place. Between the tepid and terror, there is disorientation.

I do not pretend to have a solution to our problems, a new, neatly packaged plan to escape the dilemmas of the present day. As a longtime critic of simple solutions to complex problems, as a critic of ideology, I am opposed in principle to that sort of thing. Yet I do see a range of activities with common characteristics that presents opportunities for addressing the real and pressing problems we face, and I see that the potential of this sort of action is being overlooked. This study explores the contours and potential of the "politics of small things," as such politics address the pressing concerns of our time.

I think we need to look to the details of social interaction for alternatives. Not only God, but democratic promise, is in the details. Theoretically, I propose a synthesis of the writings of Hannah Arendt and Erving Goffman. Historically, I propose a close analysis of pivotal moments in our recent past, in 1968, 1989, 2001, and 2004. Empirically, I suggest we look up close at institutions and movements to learn how spaces for democratic practices are constituted in both established and nascent democracies, as well as under modern and postmodern tyrannies.

: : :

This turn to the politics of small things, I admit, has something to do with my own experience. There was a time when my work was at the center of things, despite my intentions. I had chosen an esoteric topic for my first major research project. I studied a marginal theater movement in a small corner of the Soviet bloc. But the way the Polish student theater movement was organized in the 1970s, the sort of public it helped constitute, and the kind of expression it presented to that public, prefigured the Solidarity trade union movement, which contributed significantly to the fall of the Soviet empire and the transformation of the geopolitical world. I was studying the historical importance of the politics of small things before I thought of the notion. I will return to this study below as I try to account for the emergence of the politics of small things as an ascendant political force.

I am now drawn to small things as a way to think about politics and develop action for a number of different reasons. There is the fact that the small window of youth theater enabled me to understand the major political transformation of our times, from the inside. But beyond the personal and the idiosyncratic, there is the fact that the grand accounts of our historical circumstances have served us so poorly. The complexity of the human condition has been ignored and even repressed by such accounts, often with fatal consequences. When all history hitherto has been explained as the history of class struggle or by the laws of race, modern barbarism has been the consequence. While I do not believe that every grand theory of history and society has totalitarian potential, I think at this time we need to proceed with caution. The grandest, most complete way to oppose communism, the most radical form of anticommunism, was Nazism. The grandest, most complete way to oppose Nazism, the most radical form of antifascism, was communism. And the dangers revealed by this seem to be repeated in the struggle between the terrorists' response to American hegemony and the American response to terrorism. There is obviously little room for democracy in the project of terror and just as obviously, it seems to me, little room for democracy, at home or abroad, in the war against terror. To point out that there are smaller, less grand ways to combat powerful wrongs, I believe, is not to abdicate responsibility, but to take it. The study of the politics of small things is therefore a first step toward taking responsibility in our complex times.

I have a sense that social and political theorists are responsible for the sorry state we now live in. The terrorist does not recognize alternative, more democratic ways to pursue his or her ends. Nor does the antiterrorist. This is partially because of the inadequacies of political theory. A whole range of power is not perceived.

When people freely meet and talk to each other as equals, reveal their differences, display their distinctions, and develop a capacity to act together, they create power. Hannah Arendt distinguishes this power from coercion. It is underappreciated, both in everyday life and on the larger political stage. We will explore how this power has been constituted in our recent past, and how the potential of such power presents alternatives for action now. The fall of communism and the democratic aftermath of the fall in Central Europe were at least in part a result of this power, as were the great accomplishments of the civil rights movement and the feminist movement in the United States. This needs to be recognized.

I believe that this power must be named. Arendt developed the notion of "the lost treasure of the revolutionary tradition" to highlight the historical importance of the sort of activity I have in mind. But her tragic sense and the fact that she did not see the capacity for politics off the central political stage, as well as her elitism, led her to overlook the political significance of the free public space that is inherent in a wide range of human interactions. Such free space is to be found in workplaces and schools, government bureaucracies and corporate media institutions, and many other places in our daily lives.

: : :

I was talking to a group of students about the history of our institution, the New School for Social Research, in 1997 renamed the New School University. They were deeply concerned about this distinctive, very important, and relatively poor institution, and for good reason. Their concerns were variations on a theme common at institutions of higher learning these days. They were concerned about the logic of the bottom line replacing the logic of education, inquiry, and creativity in the institution and saw the ugly semiliterate name change as symbolic of this trend. The students came from two divisions of the New School: Parsons School of Design and the Graduate Faculty of Political and Social Science. Parsons is one of America's premier arts and design schools, established to present an alternative to the stale approach to the fine arts at the end of the nineteenth century, with the goal of connecting aesthetic concerns to the practices of a modern democratic society. The Graduate Faculty is a special social science enterprise, established in 1934 as "the University in Exile," an American response to Nazi repression. It has remained true to its tradition through the years by collaborating with democratic intellectuals who were pursuing their normative commitments despite repressive conditions in Eastern and Central Europe, Africa, and Latin America. These students were coming to understand that their two divisions had more in common than the fact that they have been integrated under the same administrative structure. They were interested in developing joint creative and scholarly projects, and were concerned that the administration did not understand their needs and would develop the university against their common interests. Then the pressing question arose: How could they flourish in the university, following their own insights, when they were powerless, when all the power was lodged in a president who was neither an academic nor an artist but a politician? To their minds, those who controlled the budget, the administration and its president, and those who had legal authority, the board of trustees, had power. They themselves did not.

When I suggested to these students that they had the power to speak to each other and develop projects in common and that this would force the administration to respond positively, they, or at least many of them, thought me a hopeless romantic. Real power involves the power of the purse and legal authority. The power of small things was just too soft, and to depend on it too softheaded. I am sure they were wrong and that the whole history of our institution, with which they were proud to be associated, belies their convictions. This was a local matter, of concern to a local audience, but it suggests to me why I must get on with this project.

The same issues present themselves throughout our social world, and nowhere are they more important than in relation to the electronic and print news media. Many critics of the media, most prominently Noam Chomsky, explain why and how these institutions support the corporate, military, and political powers.[6] Major corporations control the media, and the media as private enterprises depend upon advertising revenues for their profits. Politicians and other state agents are major news sources. The media, needing economic resources and information sources, are careful not to bite the hands that feed them, so present a view of the world that supports the interests of corporate power and the state. They hesitate in reporting news that runs counter to the interests of their sponsors and subjects, sometimes because of active political and corporate interference but probably more often because of quiet self-censorship. In either case it is a manifestation of institutional dependence and control. And the major news media corporations, as corporations, have interests that are identical to other major corporations. From the point of view of the left, there is no doubt that there is significant evidence to believe that the news is formulated in a fashion that protects the interests of corporate and state power.

Yet there is also little doubt that there is a liberal bias to the news, as Bernard Goldberg asserts.[7] The people who work in the major media view the world from the left of the center of U.S. public opinion. They are more favorably oriented to liberal pressure groups, more cosmopolitan and committed to diversity, more likely to vote for Democratic political candidates and to have more elitist cultural preferences. From the point of view of the right, the bias of the media is a result, not of corporate ownership, or of the effects of advertising, or of state pressure, but of the liberal character of the people in the newsroom.

In responding to criticisms, media professionals reassure themselves that if they are getting it both from the left and the right, they must be doing something right. But there is significantly more involved. Apart from the criticisms of the left and right, there is another, smaller story, not the result of the workings of big political economic institutions or of elitist culture. In the interactions among media professionals the stories of left and right must be qualified in a significant way.

In 1996, I participated in a conference on media and globalization in Essen, Germany. It was a gathering of critical social scientists and political and cultural theorists, for the most part leftists. I met there a broadcast journalist, a foreign reporter for ABC News. Her presentation was very much within the "Chomsky consensus" of the gathering. She expressed her deep concern that the then recent acquisition of ABC by the Walt Disney Corporation would fundamentally challenge the integrity of the news division. The narratives of the left and the right are revealed by her presence and her presentation at the conference. The way a corporate takeover could effect negatively the editorial independence of a major source of American news was revealed, from the inside, in her talk. And the liberal bias of a major media figure, a blunt critic of corporate capital, was apparent in her very person. Yet a third, mostly overlooked, narrative was also present.

The missing element is the power generated by the interactions among journalists and their critics: by the participation of the journalist in the conference, by her dealings with journalist colleagues, and, at a further remove, by the activities of conservative and radical critics of journalism. At the conference, she expressed outrage at the implications of the takeover, not because it weakened her own political position within her institution but because she felt that the objectivity of the news service would be compromised by the new corporate owner. Feeding the antiglobalization prejudices of the conference members, she publicly wondered about her capacity to report on problems at Euro Disney: Would ABC even report problems there? Would its news reports be manipulated to serve the marketing interests of the parent corporation? And would this lead to a further blurring of business interests, entertainment values, and journalistic standards? These are serious questions, but raising them is just as significant as supplying answers. The answers have to do with the power of convictions and corporations but also the power of critical reflection and action. She spoke with the conference participants and with her colleagues about these questions, and through the discussion and actions based upon them, they ratified together the long-standing expectation of journalistic independence. They defined the situation in a way that demanded independence and defined compromise of independence as repression. Their interactions may or may not have been compromised by corporate power or political conviction. The journalist and others acted upon their collectively constituted expectations. The power of small things has to be considered along with the power of big ones. ABC News may not be completely independent from the calculations of the bottom line at Disney, but when journalists act as journalists and monitor each other's actions, they put distance between the bottom line and news reporting. Chomsky and others would have us believe that there is little difference between the *New York Times* and the *Pravda* of old, but actually the difference is great, thanks to the commitment to independent professionalism created by professionals in interaction.

In interacting with each other, media professionals at least pretend to be professional, and they make the same pretense when challenged by their audience or by critics. They distinguish their partisan commitments and their institution's interests from their own commitment to delivering the news in an objective fashion. The appearance of professional standards, and professional interactions according to those standards, defines a significant social reality. When it seems that the principles are compromised, speech and action generate new professional principles. A free media, influenced as it is by economic and political pressures and by cultural dispositions, operates when professional ideals free it from these pressures, or at least make it possible to struggle against the pressures. This struggle is a small matter with very big consequences, crucial to the viability of democratic practices.

Such struggle over social definition is a key component of the politics of small things. Constituted as individuals interact with each other, it gives rise to a situational reality that is a significant political force, opening the possibility of controlling the power of the state and global corporations and checking the power of personal conviction. The power of the definition of the situation is the engine of the politics of small things.

The politics of small things has long been with us, yet in a sense it is a startling and revolutionary innovation of our times. It has always been the case that when participants in a social situation define something as being real, it is real in its consequences, as the early-twentieth-century social psychologist W. I. Thomas put it.[8] It is my contention that this power of definition has now become decisive. In this book, we will observe the politics of small things as it helped define key moments in our recent past. We will explore how the politics of small things entered the central political stage in 1968 (chapter 2), how it was a key component in the great transformations in 1989 (chapter 3), how the failure of key political actors to pay sufficient attention to its power led to tragic consequences in 2001 (chapter 4), and how in 2004 the micropolitics of the left and right became a key terrain of political conflict: in the antiwar movement and the presidential campaign of Howard Dean (chapter 5) and in the mobilization of the Christian right in local churches (chapter 6). This last conflict, I will attempt to demonstrate, was a struggle for partisan power and a struggle for democratic principle, which went beyond partisanship. We will then analyze the social construction of a politics of small things in specific social institutions of education and journalism (chapter 7). As we define the situation in virtual and embodied interactions, the power of the politics of small things is amplified and undermined on television; this is explored in chapter 8. We will conclude with a consideration of the specific political character of the power of small things in our dark times, given the interaction of the history of political culture and the formation of the media landscape.

When people talk to each other, defining a situation on their own terms and developing a capacity to act in concert, they constitute a democratic alternative to terror and hegemonic force. We know too well how the powers use the electronic media, making it seem that they are the only game in town, and we are learning all too clearly how the dramatic gestures of terrorism are amplified by global media. In this inquiry I will highlight the ways democratic actions have constituted free spaces in the global networks of the twentieth century and consider the prospects for this continuing in the twenty-first, and I will present a guide for appreciating and cultivating such prospects. Both critics and partisans of the prevailing order of things have overlooked this potential, with very dangerous results in the grand game of the terrorists and the antiterrorists. This inquiry will be an exploration of the alternatives.

1

Theorizing the Kitchen Table and Other Small Things

What we need . . . is a political philosophy that isn't erected around the problem
of sovereignty, nor therefore, around the problems of law and prohibition. We
need to cut off the king's head: in political theory that has still to be done.

Michel Foucault, "Truth and Power"

To be political, to live in a *polis*, meant that everything was decided through words
and persuasion and not through force and violence. In Greek self-understanding,
to force people by violence, to command rather than persuade, were prepolitical
ways to deal with people characteristic of life outside the *polis*. . . .

For us, appearance—something that is being seen and heard by others as well
as by ourselves—constitutes reality.

. . . The distinction between private and public coincides with the opposition of
necessity and freedom, of futility and permanence, and finally of shame and
honor. **Hannah Arendt, *The Human Condition***

Without something to belong to, we have no stable self, and yet total commitment and attachment to any social unit implies a kind of selflessness. Our sense
of being a person can come from being drawn into a wider social unit; our sense of
selfhood can arise through the little ways in which we resist the pull. Our status
is backed by the solid buildings of the world, while our sense of personal identity often resides in the cracks.

Erving Goffman, "The Underlife of a Public Institution"

: : :

As we embark on our exploration of the grounds for an alternative to the politics of despair and terror, I must clarify

what I mean by the politics of small things. I do not have in mind micro-interaction in general, nor all attempts at acting locally while thinking globally. Rather, I want to highlight something built into the social fabric, by active people, a potential component of everyday life. In this chapter, I will demonstrate what I mean by presenting three snapshots of the politics of small things, discuss how the events they depict contributed to one of the major transformations of our times, and interpret the snapshots from the theoretical viewpoint of three major social theorists. This will set a theoretically informed stage for the subsequent historical and empirical investigation.

Snapshots of the Politics of Small Things

Our first picture is of a general but significant location: the kitchen table in Poland and elsewhere in the old bloc. During the Soviet period, small circles of intimate friends were able to talk to each other without concern for the present party line around the kitchen table. This free zone, where one could speak one's mind without concern about the interaction between the official and the unofficial, produced unusually warm and intense ties among family and friends. Here Communist Party members would complain about "them," meaning the party, without consciousness of contradiction. Here personal and collective memories were told and retold in opposition to official history. This was the private place that was most remote from official mandates and controls, although in the worst of times, attempts were made to invade even this space, as children were called upon to denounce their parents. A keen appreciation of this private space begins to explain, for example, the initially good-humored wariness toward feminism on the part of women (and men) from the former Soviet bloc.[1] Any denigration of private space was viewed with suspicion. Any attempt to make private questions political seemed exactly wrong.

: : :

The shield and lessons of this privacy, with its free interaction, did expand public freedom. A private apartment in a typical socialist housing bloc, for example, became a bookstore of illegal literature. Nothing about the apartment suggested that this was a commercial establishment. Its owner was a bibliomaniac whose passion, widespread in intellectual circles, was to buy and read everything published, officially or unofficially, on controversial themes. Officially he was an educational researcher, in fact he was a bookseller. He pretended to work and they pretended to pay him, as the old joke went.

Books, to him and many others like him, were prize possessions, indicating where people stood in the cultural and political world. This attitude was not uncommon, but there was something uncommon about this apartment. One approached it with first a brief telephone call and then a ring on the doorbell. The door opened. Polite regards from a mutual friend were exchanged, followed by a query concerning the latest number of an underground publication. It was available and produced for the customer. The price was stated, then paid. The buyer and seller acted like buyer and seller. They were not oppositionist heroes. This was the everyday life of the opposition, which included a nice profit for "bookstores," and for publishers and writers.

: : :

In another apartment we find a poetry reading, "Walendowski's Salon." The atmosphere here was one of much greater tension. Weekly, in this unusually large Warsaw apartment, intellectuals and artists met for unofficial readings, lectures, and discussions. Monthly, with only some irregularity, there were interventions by the authorities, ranging from physical harassment to arrests. On this day, a famous actress was reading the poetry of a well-known dissident, Stanislaw Baranczak. Two weeks earlier, a number of students exiting the apartment had been severely beaten.

Nonetheless, the reading was a decidedly normal affair. Before the show began, people socialized as at a large party or in the lobby of a theater during intermission. Old friends exchanged pleasantries and gossip, new participants were introduced. I met some very famous dissidents and some young students who were new to the scene. One thing was striking in all the interactions. The people there conducted themselves as they would at any cultural gathering. When a famous professor or independent intellectual figure came in, the less famous maneuvered to get a good look and perhaps enter into a momentary conversation, all the while affecting the studied nonchalance necessary to show one belonged. They watched, and emulated, the bearing of the renowned. The audience for the reading, as is usual, worked at both appreciating the recited words and signaling to each other that they appreciated them. There was a studied normality to their interactions, intended to show themselves and each other that they were not engaged in a political (i.e., anti-Party) activity,

even though the authorities would define it as such, using the official ideological frame of definition.

: : :

These are snapshots drawn from my memory. There are thousands of others, which also reveal the interactive constitution of an emerging alternative public and politics within previously existing socialism in the 1970s
and '80s.[2] Taken together, they tell a story of political transformation.
These small events contributed to the transformation—indeed, the transformation could not have happened without them. The major theories
of transformation draw upon these little lessons, centering on the revived
appreciation of civil society. The major strategy of Solidarity applied
them. In these snapshots, the relation between interactive dimensions of a
free public is revealed, having very much to do with the relation between
politics and truth. Erving Goffman, Hannah Arendt, and Michel Foucault
can help us understand these dimensions and relationships.

Theoretical Perspectives

Erving Goffman was one of the great sociologists of the twentieth century. He analyzed and described how people presented themselves in
everyday life and through that presentation constituted social reality.
Looming behind his account of the normal life of civil society, though,
was the life of those in total institutions, where such presentation is taken
out of people's hands and they are destroyed as independent selves,
robbed of the capacity to make their social reality.

Arendt was a great political thinker of the twentieth century who considered the human condition in dark times, reflecting upon the experiences of the past and imagining possible futures, trying to understand the
confusions of her present, confusions which tragically included the horrors of modern tyranny, of totalitarianism, the origins of which she tried
to analyze, the phenomenology of which she tried to describe. She understood that the alternative to totalitarianism was to be found in man's
political capacity, the capacity to appear and speak in the presence of others, as an equal, based upon the principle of freedom. The power of politics she understood as opposed to coercion, as the capacity for people to
act in concert. The interaction between people is for Arendt, as it is for
Goffman, "where the action is."

Foucault was also a major thinker of our recent past. He too was interested in everyday actions and interactions. But for him the central

question is not about situational definitions (Goffman) or freedom (Arendt) but about discipline. He wanted to understand how power, both of words and deeds, disciplined and punished, accounting for what has been uniquely modern. Freedom and enlightenment are not definitive of the modern age for Foucault. The modern, rather, is a unique regime of truth and power. When he calls for a new sort of political theory, he proposes to study not freedom but its opposite.

Toward the end of his life, however, Foucault became concerned with his relationship with the Enlightenment and the role of the intellectual in the contemporary age. It is in his reflections on these issues that Foucault seemed to try to account for his own free agency as a political actor, and for the role of critique and critical action in the contemporary social order.

These three thinkers worked separately. Although Arendt and Goffman were contemporaries, there is no evidence that they read each other's works. And Foucault makes only passing references to his predecessors. Still, they do speak to each other in interesting ways, and the exchange illuminates the elusive domain we are attempting to understand.

Seeking an understanding of the domain of the politics of small things, I will (1) present a synthesis of Arendt and Goffman on freedom and (2) contrast Goffman-Arendt with Foucault on political culture, which will lead to (3) a sharp contrast between Goffman-Arendt and Foucault on the politics of everyday life. This latter contrast I take to have crucial political significance. It will give clear definition to the politics of small things. We embark upon these theoretical steps by closely analyzing the three snapshots of everyday life.

The Snapshots in Theoretical Perspective

In each of the snapshots—of the kitchen table, the apartment bookstore, and the underground salon—power is enacted, revealing the subject of political theory as a site with the "king's head cut off," as Foucault would have it. The regime of truth of socialism is nonetheless present in the daily lives of its subjects. At the kitchen table, friends and relatives are relatively free to discuss narratives of their lives that are distinct from the official truth. Yet they must take into account that truth as they move beyond the table, and this they must be aware of and discuss. Adults discuss the meaning of the latest twists and turns of party policy and how it will effect their lives. Children are taught what can be said only at home. The official rendering of the order of things is taken for granted, just part of life.

While power does not directly intervene in these interactions among friends and family, it is present. It controls even what is articulated against the powers. The distance from the party state and its official demands may be understood as a distancing from power, creating space for discussion and reflection. But it is also the case that public compliance with the official order is insured in the interactions that occur around the table. Most people are aware of the existence of dissidents, as they are publicized as rogue elements in the official press. If they didn't exist, the state would have to create them.[3]

At the bookstore and in the literary salon much more is present: alternative literatures and arts, alternative political and social programs. But these too are channeled, hidden. And those who are not actively committed, know that their presence excites disciplinary responses from the regime.

These elements of the snapshots might have been part of an account Foucault would have given, an account that emphasizes the intimate connection between power and knowledge. The official knowledge, its truth and its power, disciplines those around the kitchen table, and it is very evident in the bookstore and the salon. It encloses different ways of doing things and assures that they are held in check. The escalating critical task is to disengage the truth from the specific truth regime.

Arendt would present a very different view. For her, appearances are realities, and that which does not appear is politically insignificant. The household and the public sphere are distinct locations in the Athenian world: the former, the realm of necessity, the latter, the realm of freedom. But something changes in the totalitarian context. The "origins of totalitarianism" is a story of the destruction of public space to the point that the totalitarian order is without any public space. The snapshots, though, disclose a public capacity within the private arena. Beyond the kitchen table, people cannot appear openly, speak to each other, and defend their freedom. But around the table, they do just that. They can tell each other stories about what is happening in the wider world, can add critical commentary, and discuss alternative courses of action in their lives and the lives of their compatriots.

The bookstore and the salon further develop this public space in which critical reflection and independent creation can appear. The general principle of action around the kitchen table is now extended beyond the bonds of intimate trust, to the written word and its distribution and to the spoken word. People appear before each other, speak to each other, and develop capacities to act in concert. They create alternative institutions and these institutions develop. The buyer and the seller in the bookstore meet each other and in a small way contribute to the development of an alternative literary public sphere in Poland. When we think of the great dissident movements of the former Soviet bloc, we think of the heroes of the center stage, of Sakharov, Solzhenitsyn, Brodsky, Havel, Michnik, Kuron, and other such figures. But these heroes acted with the support of others who helped constitute interactive supports for their actions. The buyers and sellers of illegal books, and the way they bought and sold the books, sustained the action of heroes. Arendt focused on the heroes and did not adequately understand the social constitution of heroism. But it was very much there and supported the principles that most concerned her.

When friends and relatives met in their kitchens, they presented themselves to each other in such a way that they defined the situation in terms of an independent frame rather than that of officialdom. Clear social rituals were observed. Almost immediately, they would ask each other about the latest jokes. They would exchange bits of information about the doings of the powers that might suggest the direction of things to come. Then there would be singing, of folk songs, popular tunes, and sarcastic renditions of Stalinist agit-prop songs from the late 1940s and early 1950s. Intimate grammatical forms were the rule. When "newspeak," the public language, the language of officialdom, was spoken, it was with a raised eyebrow or distancing tone. In this way friendship was forged and a general orientation established. Bonds of trust developed, enabling each individual who took part to forge an identity, a self, that was strikingly different from his or her institutionally defined persona. This was public life hidden in a private space. It was a space defined as outside the frame of party ideology, a space wherein a countervailing frame was developed. In this way, we can understand the snapshots through the sociology of Goffman.

The bookstore represented an expansion of the type of relations found in such intimate settings, creating social bonds that went further beyond the family. The friendship rituals developed in kitchen table meetings were the grounds upon which the bookstore was socially constructed. A buyer and seller may or may not have met around the kitchen table, but at least they could refer to mutual acquaintances whom they knew in this capacity. They exchanged greetings in a quick and clipped fashion and quickly inquired about their acquaintances, affirming the mutual trust forged in friendship circles, and then moved on to the business at hand. The exchange was illegal, of course, but they affected an air of studied normality, acting with a coolness that would be appropriate when buying a newspaper at the local kiosk. They were not conspiring against the state. They were engaged in a business transaction that should have been an open and everyday practice. Acting as if they lived in a free society, they were creating a regularized pattern of social interaction, an institution in fact, which was a component part of a free civil society.

This interactive constitution of a free civil society was yet more apparent in the literary gathering, where strangers, not just friends and mutual acquaintances, met to take part in an independent cultural event. Through ritual practices of deference and demeanor, the dignity of public actors was confirmed, and their relationship with others was marked out. A private apartment was thus defined by the event's participants as a public theater, a public forum, and because they presented themselves accordingly, a real public forum was constituted. The powers were there in that everyone knew they could put an end to the event with a police action. But short of such brute intervention, their interactions formed a free public space of the sort Arendt described. And exactly such institutions, by the end of the 1980s, brought down the repressive force, which was backed by the military might of a superpower.

Culture and Power and Public Interaction

By presenting themselves to each other as free and independent social agents, the people who gathered around kitchen tables, in illegal bookstores, and in independent cultural institutions created a free public domain such as Hannah Arendt described. Her description involves an idea about political power and political culture which is strikingly different from most conventional understandings, and which strikingly contrasts with Michel Foucault's position.

Foucault analyzes the problem of knowledge and power—the problem of the truth regime, as he puts it. Truth, in his view, is a production of institutions and their discourses. It produces power and is controlled by it. There is no distance between truth and the powers, but there are alternative powers with alternative truths. Foucault explains: "It is not a matter of emancipating truth from every system of power (which would be a chimera, for *truth is already power*) but of detaching truth from the forms of hegemony, social, economic, and cultural, within which it operates at the present time."[4] The analytic task is to explore truth regimes. The critical task is to do the "detaching." The people around the kitchen table who move first to the bookstore and then the literary salon can be understood as engaging in this sort of bodily detachment. But what is the value of it? Why choose one truth regime over another? Foucault does not explain. Arendt, though, is critically suggestive in answering just these questions.

Arendt maintains that there are two fundamentally different types of truth, factual and philosophical, which have two very different relationships to political power. Factual truth (which is not part of Foucault's scheme) must be the grounds upon which a free politics (again, not part of Foucault's scheme) is based. Philosophical truth must be radically separated from politics, a possibility Foucault denies. Arendt's distinctions are made to facilitate an understanding of the nature of totalitarianism and its alternatives. This is crucial for the present inquiry, both for scholarly and for normative reasons. The existence of alternatives centers on the constitution of public freedom and the possibilities of a democratic culture, both of which are constituted in and through the domain of a free public. While Foucault cannot distinguish between totalitarianism and liberalism, Arendt reveals how, in the relationship between truth and power, this crucial distinction is made.

In order to make the contrast between the two different types of truth clear, Arendt reflects upon the beginning of World War I. The causes of the war are open to interpretation. The aggressive intentions of Central Powers or the Allies can be emphasized, as can the intentional or unanticipated consequences of political alliances. The state of capitalism and imperialism in crisis may be understood as being central. Yet when it comes to the border of Belgium, it is factually the case that Germany invaded Belgium and not the other way around. A free politics cannot be based on an imposed interpretation. There must be an openness to opposing views. But a free politics also cannot be based on a factual lie, such as the proposition that Belgium's invasion of Germany opened World War I. Modern liberal democracy requires a separation of politics from philosophical truth, but it must be based upon factual truths in order for those who meet in public to share a common world in which they can interact politically. Modern tyranny is based on a kind of philosophical truth, an ideology, an official interpretation of the facts; factual truth is, as a matter of principle, expendable. When Arendt highlights Trotsky as a kind of totalitarian everyman in *The Origins of Totalitarianism,* she observes that he expresses his fealty to the truth of the Communist Party.[5] But the fact that he could be airbrushed out of the history of the Bolshevik revolution, contrary to the factual truth—that he was a key figure, commander of the Red Army, second only to Lenin—is also definitive of totalitarianism.[6] This is the real cultural ground of political correctness, of official truth. The Party's purportedly scientific understanding of history substitutes for political confrontation, debate, and deliberation and is enforced by terror. Our scenes from the democratic opposition each involved attempts by social actors to free themselves from the official truth and to ground themselves in the factual truth. We will observe how this worked in the specific historical context in the next two chapters.

From the point of view of Foucault, or, for that matter, from the point of view of the sociology of knowledge and culture, there is much that is unsatisfying about Arendt's position. The distinction between fact and interpretation, which she insists upon, is in practice hard to maintain, and empirically it is hard to discern. But this is not the telling point from Arendt's point of view. Rather, it is that the distinction needs to be *pursued,* so that a free public life can be *constituted.* A democratic public cannot be constituted if political questions are answered philosophically, nor can its citizens interact freely, speak and act in the presence of each other, if their interactions are based upon state-imposed lies.

The politics of race in America could not proceed democratically if a politically correct standard of racial interaction were actually imposed. (This is of course far from occurring, given the popularity of critics of political correctness.) Nor could a democratic confrontation of the legacies of racial injustice in the United States proceed if the young were taught in school that blacks had owned whites, rather than the other way around. For a free public life to exist, there needs to be space for speech and actions based upon different opinions; then the people, and not the theorists, philosophers, historians, or scientists, can rule. But their rule can proceed on solid grounds only if they share a political world together, which has some factual solidity.

Factual truth is the bedrock of a free politics. Difference of interpretation and opinion is its process. That the factual sometimes fades into the interpretive does not mitigate against the requirement that an interpretive scheme or doctrine cannot substitute for politics. That the interpretive sometimes seems to the convinced to be the factual does not mitigate against the requirement that for people to meet and interact in a free public, they must share a sense of a factual world. That fact and interpretation get mixed up is very much a part of the messiness of politics, a messiness that is confronted in concrete interactive situations. This points us in Goffman's direction, which we will turn to intensively in the analyses of institutions and movements later in our inquiry. For now, we need to consider a bit more closely Arendt's position, so that the historical context of our inquiry can be understood.

When Arendt first presented her diagnosis, the central critical thrust of her work involved her identification of the National Socialism of Germany with Soviet communism. Although according to traditional political categories, these regimes appeared to be opposites, one of the right and the other of the left, she underscored that in their use of ideology and terror, in their mode of governance, in their projects of total control, their similarities were much more important than their differences. They were regimes systematically organized to eliminate a free public life (her central normative concern). While *The Origins of Totalitarianism* can be read as a "dialectic of the Enlightenment" minus the teleology,[7] it is also an account of the destruction of free public space in political life. Arendt presents a sort of decline and fall of public life, or as Richard Sennett has put it, a story of "the fall of public man."[8] Her story of decline and fall takes the reader from the heights of antiquity to the depths of totalitarianism.

She starts with her classical utopia. Pre-Socratic Greece represents for her the time when freedom beyond necessity flourished in the polis.

> The Greek polis once was precisely that "form of government" which provided men with a space of appearances where they could act, with a kind of theater where freedom could appear. . . . If, then, we understand the political in the sense of the polis, its end or *raison d'etre* would be to establish and keep in existence a space where freedom as virtuosity can appear. This is the realm where freedom is a worldly reality, tangible in words which can be heard, in deeds which can be seen, and in events which can be talked about, remembered, and turned into stories before they are finally incorporated into the great storybook of human history.[9]

The history of Western thought, for Arendt, is the history of the decline of the appreciation of this utopia, with catastrophic consequences in modernity. The Greek turn to political philosophy meant that the philosopher—in contemporary language, the intellectual—sought to substitute the truth for political governance. The Christian identification of freedom with free will turned freedom into a private and not a public matter. This confusion of public and private, from Arendt's point of view, explains the identification of freedom with sovereignty as articulated by such thinkers as Hobbes and Rousseau.[10] Structurally this is manifest in the rise of society, in which she sees the public and the private confused as a matter of principle.[11] Modernity intensified this loss of a distinctively political capacity, even as independent democratic and republican political forms were invented. Arendt notes, with approval, the Anglo-American conception of the political party, especially as defended by Edmund Burke. Competing parties presented alternative notions of the common good. Continental parties serving the interests of particular classes, she understands as movements that confuse particular interests with the public good, the interests of property, real and capital, and the interests of labor, rural and urban, with the interests of the public.[12] "Anti-

Semitism," "Imperialism," and "Totalitarianism," the three parts of *The Origins of Totalitarianism,* each analyze developments that destroy political capacity, as the phenomena they name are central to the history of European civilization. Totalitarian movements and regimes are the culmination of this story of radical depoliticization.

Arendt argues that what is distinctive about totalitarianism is its unique conflation of culture and coercion, ideology and terror.[13] The problem with her position is that it requires what appear to be utopian beliefs about the relationship between truth and politics: that interpretive truth and politics can be radically separated and that factual truth can be the basis of politics. While her critique of the substitution of philosophy for politics may be cogent, and while it may be crucial for intellectuals and artists not to mistake their insights and imaginations for democratic deliberation and decision,[14] her ideas about the separation of politics from interpretive truth may still seem unrealistic. Every political movement, after all, has its ideology.[15] Further, it is unclear how to maintain this separation while maintaining a commitment to factual truth. In these postmodern times, we are very much aware that one person's interpretation is another's factual truth. Indeed, the sociology of knowledge, at least since Mannheim, points in the same direction. It would seem that Foucault with his ideas about truth regimes is on the empirical mark. Yet, as I have already tried to demonstrate, there is a normative problem with Foucault's position. He cannot distinguish between Leon Trotsky and Woodrow Wilson, between a totalitarian and a liberal. Further, there are also empirical grounds for rejecting the Foucaultian position.

This is where small things matter. It is a question of appearances, of working to sustain realities. Truth and politics, knowledge and power, do not have a general relationship in modernity, as Foucault maintains. Rather, as we have already noted, social agents constitute the relationship in concrete interactive situations. The authorities of the Soviet bloc tried to maintain an ideological definition of the situation, conflating knowledge and power. They presented an official truth and demanded that people appear to follow its edicts. In official space people pretended to believe the official ideology, but around the kitchen table, in the independent bookstore, and at the literary salon the imposed relationship was questioned.

Around the kitchen table people dropped pretense. They appeared in a different guise. They constituted a clandestine public space where they could speak and act together, free of the demands of officialdom. A real escalation of the struggle against the official order became evident when this hidden space of free interaction openly appeared. The patterns of interaction, including the rituals of deference and demeanor evident in Walendowski's Salon, were framed not by the official ideology but by a distancing from ideological definition. The interaction appeared more like the interaction around the kitchen table than that at an official gathering. Foucault would explain this development in a sort of value-neutral way. One truth regime, that of dissidents, was emerging from another. Perhaps, we would even go so far as to say that the regime of the new hegemonic order of globalization could be observed in the detaching of embodied practices from the truths, that is the ideology, of the old regimes. Note how much more we observe using the theory of Arendt, informed by Goffman.

The Political Culture of the Politics of Small Things

In the positions of Foucault and Arendt, we observe two distinct understandings of political culture, two different ways of understanding the relationships between knowledge and power, truth and politics. While both get us beyond the lazy use of stereotype (all Russians seek a strong central authority, Americans are flexible, the British are more formal, the French more rational), they do so with very different formulations. Where Foucault sees an identity, Arendt sees a variable relationship. For Foucault, political culture is about truth regimes, about the particular way that power and knowledge are united. For Arendt, political culture is about how and how far power and culture are distinguished and related. As we saw when reflecting upon the snapshots of the Polish democratic opposition, both analytic approaches provide insights into important aspects of political experience.

In fact, I am not sure that we can decide which one is more accurate. Foucault reveals an important part of the story that is generally not sufficiently appreciated. The powers are revealed as operating in the activities of daily life, and there is a form of knowledge that both accounts for this and makes it difficult to inspect critically. Knowledge and truth discipline. But, Arendt forcefully maintains, there are different kinds of truth and they have different relationships with power, or politics. This is a critique of Foucault's position, but more significantly, it highlights a domain that Foucault ignores. The political implication of this is great. It means that there is a domain for freedom which Foucault does not recognize. This provides the grounds for normative judgment, making it possible to contrast tyranny with freedom.

Arendt provides the general position. In the snapshots, we saw how judgment becomes part of everyday interaction. We also considered the interactive sociology of Goffman. The people around the kitchen table, in the bookstore, and at the salon constituted freedom in their interactions, as they distinguished factual and philosophical truth. They created a free politics of small things. This dimension of politics and culture must be understood as an ongoing activity, in process. It is not inevitable or a working out of well-conceived philosophical positions. It is actively constituted.

Now we are prepared to turn to this creative act as it played a key role in pivotal moments in our recent past: 1968, 1989, 2001, and 2004. We will move not only through time but also through space, from face-to-face interaction to virtual interaction, from the Eastern Europe of the former Soviet bloc to the global setting of terrorism, antiterrorism, and anti-antiterrorism. As we proceed, we will be making a lot of comparisons, a lot of contrasts, but there is an underlying goal: an appreciation of a neglected dimension of politics and its historical significance.

2 1968: Theater of Truth

Arendt tells us that in politics appearances are realities, and Goffman explores how we maintain appearances to create social and individual realities. He shows that in human interaction in modern complex societies competing possible definitions of the situation in the greater society are worked out through framing. Only in total institutions, asylums and prisons and the like, are alternative frames almost eliminated, and even in these he explores how inmates create free zones for independent action and self-definition. We have seen how the politics of framing presented itself in the everyday life of Soviet-bloc socialism. Interactions there constituted, in ever more open circumstances, a free public life, and this crucially involved addressing the problems of truth and politics in the way Arendt specifies. Now let's look at how this happened historically. The pivotal year is 1968.

Nineteen sixty-eight is remembered as a year of pivotal change in political culture in France, Japan, Mexico, Germany, and the United States, among many other places. The Vietnam war was challenged in the U.S. and abroad. Authoritarian political and cultural institutions were attacked everywhere and reformed in some places. In other places, notably Mexico City, brutal repression was used to defend the status quo, but even so change was initiated. Some changes occurred almost immediately, as in the educational institutions in France and Germany; elsewhere it took years (the shift in American public opinion about the war) or even decades (the transformation of Mexican politics). This year has been much studied and is recalled nostalgically by many. Yet in my judgment, some of the most telling events set into motion during that most eventful of years have not been adequately considered for their theoretical importance. I have in mind events that transpired behind the "iron curtain." The snapshots presented in chapter 1 occurred on a stage set by these events of '68.

The tragedy of the Prague Spring is of course remembered: Dubcek's socialism with a human face, the hope that existing socialism could be reformed from above, that a more dynamic economy could be introduced, along with freedom of expression and perhaps even competitive elections, all ending with the incursion of Soviet tanks. The events in Warsaw and their aftermath have been less broadly considered. In those events, we can observe up close the microculture of axial political change, the constitution of public life through social interaction. In such interaction, the necessarily complicated relationship between truth and politics was reasserted and a free public life was created as an alternative to the totalitarian relationship.[1]

: : :

The events in Poland were sparked by the closing of a play, Adam Mickiewicz's *Dziady* ("Forefather's Eve"). On January 30, 1968, Kazimierz Dejmek's production of this nineteenth-century classic at the National Theater was closed down by order of the Ministry of Culture. At the last performance, the house was overflowing. The audience reportedly included cultural figures who had returned from abroad in a show of solidarity with the theater company. Those without tickets sat in the aisles and on the edges of balconies. Students packed the theater, responding to notices nailed to doors at Warsaw University, urging a large turnout.

The play includes anticzarist lines: "We Poles have sold our souls for a couple of silver rubles [and] the only thing Moscow sends us are jackasses, idiots, and spies." The audience responded strongly to these lines. While it is not clear whether the production was intended as a criticism of Soviet domination, it is clear that in the interaction between performers and audience historical lines were turned into commentary on contemporary events. Here we observe one of the very exciting characteristics of theater, as opposed to film, the fact that the qualities of a performance, and even its meaning, are determined in the interaction between performer and audience. The politics of small things is a constituent element of theater.

This characteristic makes theater a distinctively social art form, and points to the small things that are constitutive of political order and change.

Immediately following the performance, the bounds of politics expanded beyond the walls of the theater, as two hundred students marched to a nearby statue of Mickiewicz (itself a symbol of Polish independence), denouncing the closing of the play. They were met there by the Peoples Militia. When the students refused to disperse, a number were arrested. On February 29, the Warsaw section of the official Polish Writers' Union refused to back a Communist Party proposal condemning the student protests, and instead adopted a proposal condemning the closing of *Dziady*.

On March 9, four thousand students demonstrated on the grounds of Warsaw University, demanding the reinstatement of two students who had been expelled as a consequence of their participation in the play. Violent clashes with the militia followed, with students chanting, "No study without freedom!" "We want *Dziady*!" "Long live the writers!" Dozens of students were arrested. The protests spread. Students clashed with the militia at universities throughout Poland. Everywhere they protested the closing of *Dziady* and expressed solidarity with the Prague Spring, which was then in full swing.

The response of those in power in Poland and those in the Soviet embassy, beyond that of ordinary Polish theatergoers, gave decisive definition to the performance's meaning. The powers quite apparently deemed the production and the audience's response to it as inappropriate, an anti-Soviet manifestation, and ordered the closing of the play.

The generation of political meaning through the give and take between actors and audience and in the movement of people in and out of the theater creatively constituted public space. The powers tried to stifle this and succeeded, but only in the short term. This highlights the fact that social differentiation and the sustained interaction based on differentiation constitute the public space of civil society. People hold different positions in civil society. They understand the world differently, as they interact. They confront each other in public space. Recognizing their differences, they conflict. They compromise. They prevail. They succumb. They live the life of a free civil society. This kind of normality was appearing in Poland in 1968. Something new was emerging in People's Poland that would only for a while be overshadowed by the central political stage.

The events of '68, as they came to be known in Poland, ended with an infamous anti-Zionist, antiliberal campaign. A slogan frequently chanted by students throughout the country was revealing: "Down with Moczar." This pointed to a larger political struggle that lay behind the events. There was in fact a three-way political dance in progress among (1) the writers, students, and theater company, (2) the First Secretary of the Communist Party, Wladyslaw Gomulka, and (3) General Moczar and the "partisans," ultranationalists within the Communist Party, who were pushing an anti-Semitic, anti-Zionist campaign and challenging Gomulka for party leadership. At the time, the challenge of the liberal students, writers, and theater people was frontally repressed, and it seemed that the significant action was in the conflict between the relatively moderate and reactionary wings of the party. Moczar accused Gomulka, whose wife was Jewish, of insufficient anti-Zionism, that is, he played the Polish anti-Semitic card. Gomulka outflanked him by himself ordering an anti-Semitic purge of the political and cultural leadership. In the official press, Jews were "outed." One could read newspaper stories in which Kowalik's real name was revealed to be Schwartz, in which it was explained that he was obviously not sufficiently Polish. The elite drama played itself out. Gomulka managed to hold on to power for two more years but in 1970 was overthrown by a technocratic wing of the party.

While the immediate political struggles were of only transient importance (since the collapse of communism throughout the Soviet bloc, the factional conflicts back then seem trivial), fundamental changes of political culture were emerging, although not yet clearly visible. These have had much more enduring significance. The linking of the various demands, going beyond the attempts of various forms of "socialism with a human face" and "humanistic Marxism," created a new independent public in Poland. The continuation of this discussion and its informal and sometimes clandestine institutionalization through 1989 distinguished the quality of the opposition to communism in Poland. The interactions pointed beyond theater walls and ultimately beyond the controversies of · that immediate time.

The Rediscovery of Public Freedom

That an axial change has occurred in the last two decades is well known, although its interpretation is very much contested: After 1989, after the fall of the Berlin Wall, the cold war came to an end. Soviet communism collapsed. Socialism no longer appeared viable as a systemic alternative to capitalism. Democracy became the modern political ideal, without rival. Capitalism was triumphant. History ended. Globalization began. American hegemony became the clear and present danger. These are among many ways of describing the change. Each situates a political position and guides practical action. The political spectrum has been reformulated through and with these competing interpretations. The culture

of political debate is now formed by the way the revolution in the political landscape is accounted for. But beyond such debate, and, in fact, before it, lies a rediscovery of public freedom as an interactive process.

The rediscovery of public freedom as a principle is the key to understanding the recent axial change. There is a sense in which this rediscovery began with the 1968 performances of *Dziady* at the Polish National
Theater and became a part of the democratic opposition in the 1970s, first
in Poland and then in much of Central Europe. With the rise of the Polish union Solidarność (Solidarity) in the 1980s, it became a world-historic
oppositional force, both above- and underground, culminating with the
collapse of communism, as well as democratic transitions in Latin America, Africa, Eastern and Central Europe, the former Soviet Union, and
Asia. The sequence is not the crucial point of the account I am suggesting. Rather it is the interactive constitution of public life and its culture,
the centrality of the politics of small things.

There is a big picture, suggested by the competing interpretations already highlighted. And there is a little picture, centered on the interper-
sonal experience of the challenges and changes in our political world,
captured in our snapshots of life around the kitchen table and the presentation of self and others in two Warsaw apartments. There is the political
drama of everyday life. Slowly the capacity to address the public good in
the presence of others, in speech and in actions, spread beyond the control of the party state, and, most significantly, this capacity became the
end of oppositional action. The principle and the actions based upon it
had nothing to do with, were set apart from, official ideology. This constituted a newly appreciated kind of power, which gave new shape to our
geopolitical world. Consider some relatively small interaction settings as
they move toward global transformation.

Embedded Autonomy

The National Theater, which presented the controversial production of
Dziady, was one of many theaters covertly challenging the official truth.
Indeed, it was one of many officially supported cultural institutions that
used party-state support but challenged official control. There was, for
example, a set of youth theaters that also operated in this way.[2] In officially supported cultural institutions, a primary norm of interaction was
a strong commitment to the autonomy of cultural imagination and action. People acted as if this norm were real, and it was real in its consequences. One of the reasons why it is now unclear whether *Dziady* was
an intentional provocation is the strong antipolitical ethos in the cultural

worlds of Eastern and Central European theater and the arts. The production's director, Kazimierz Dejmek, has denied that he purposively produced an anti-Soviet play. He took a piece of Polish classical literature, assigned reading in Polish high schools, and presented it in a fresh and original fashion. Anticzarism is a historical fact, but his purpose was to produce fine theater, not anti-Soviet propaganda. To suggest otherwise is to confuse his profession with that of a hack politician. There is a conceit in such a defense, well known to artists who write between the lines. But sometimes it is the reading that goes between the lines rather than the writing. Thus the controversy persists.

Consider further a work of the student theater movement just mentioned. Akademia Ruchu (the Academy of Movement) was in the late 1970s and '80s one of the leading experimental theaters in Poland. It was officially supported and controlled. As the group's name suggests, it experimented in movement. Some of its most innovative work occurred on the street, legally at times, illegally at others. The group played a continual cat-and-mouse game with the local Warsaw authorities and the militia. Its work ranged from the relatively innocuous, unfurling colorful cloths in stylized dances on the sidewalks and in trams, to the provocative, forming a line out of a meat store, mirroring the long ones waiting to get in to make difficult and rare purchases.

During one of its street performances, members of the militia approached them. Wojciech Krukowski, the director of the academy, showed the officials the cameras he was using to film the happenings. He explained to them that his group was making a film. Recognizing that film is controlled not in the filming but after final editing, the militia then helped the film crew get on with its work, redirecting traffic, giving the film crew the necessary conditions to finish its project. This went on for days. The militiamen thus became performers in an unauthorized street-theater performance.

Krukowski first informed me of these events in the 1980s. In a conversation we had in 1994, he completed his account. He had by then become director of Warsaw's major museum of contemporary art and had had occasion to meet with the militia official whom he had apparently misled into supporting his street-theater productions. The cop shared with the avant-garde director how he used to enjoy being "fooled" by Krukowski, how he had always understood the theater's subterfuge and supported it. Not only do creators and audiences learn how to read between the lines, so do their censors. The militia official was willing to support Akademia Ruchu in its work as long as he could deny the fact that he was doing so. People on the street and members of the militia, along with the theater group, created a momentary public space. Its independence from official control was its most important product.

Such interactive gaming was not only a theatrical matter. There was a built-in tension in all social, cultural, and political institutions within the socialist order. Officially defined as socialist, all spheres of life were subjected to ideological direction and control. But the socialist vision was also a modern one. Institutions were required to serve not only an ideological role but also an instrumental function. Farms may have been collectivized as part of an ideological script, but they still had to produce food. The great industrial works served as monuments to socialist power and the power of the working class, but they still had to produce steel, tractors, and tanks. Educational institutions still had to prepare the next generation for practical tasks, just as hospitals cared for the sick and families for the young. There was an inherent conflict between such ordinary social practices and ideology. Where the demands of these practices ended and the demands of ideology began would always be uncertain, a matter of conflict. Censorship and the political police were thus a necessary part of the official order. This is the structural, macro view of the matter. The micro view, the view of the politics of small things, suggests how fluid the situation could and did become.

Social interaction required a negotiation between orientations toward and commitments to social practices and to ideology. Parents decided how their viewpoints and memories, outside official script, would be taught around the kitchen table. Around the same tables, discussions among friends would be more or less cautious. In more formal settings, educators, industrial workers and managers, scientists, and clerks all had to go through the same face-to-face negotiations. The result from one country to another and from one period in time to another varied considerably.[3]

Vaclav Havel's classic essay "The Power of the Powerless" presents an examination of this dimension of everyday life under socialism, as he considers the potential for resistance.[4] The most famous character in this essay is a greengrocer. Havel speculates about what would happen to the grocer if he did not display the sign reading "Workers of the World Unite" along with the fruit and vegetables in his shop window, what would happen if his shop window became just that and not also a location for ideological dissemination. Havel considers all the consequences for the grocer, the loss of all privileges, but he also considers what would happen if the grocer and those around him together tried "living in truth," living apart from imposed official ideological definition. He suggested, in the mid-1970s, that it would spell the collapse of communism. This proved to be a telling insight.

A less well known character in Havel's essay demonstrates the degree to which living in truth was interwoven into daily life. Havel recalls working in a brewery where there was one brewer who really knew and was committed to his work—a master craftsman. Because he expressed more concern for the quality of the product than for party instructions concerning the solidarity of the working class and the building of socialism, his career languished while others' advanced. And when he publicly refused to compromise the quality of his work and the product, he lost his job. Ideology and normal productive practice clashed, and a dedicated worker suffered.

The choices the brewer faced were not that different from the office politics well known outside of totalitarian contexts. Although in this case the office politics was linked to the master politics of the party state, the situation is not that exotic. We all know that people who play the corporate script well often flourish, while those who do their job do not. The "office players" do the expressive work that keeps an institution functioning and are rewarded for it.

In the specific totalitarian situation, Havel is telling us, these normal dynamics serve the party state. He is concerned with two consequences, beyond personal tragedy. Because the problem is systemic and not local, there is a general compromise in the quality of work throughout the society. The logic of party ideology is so fundamentally opposed to the logic of good work—no matter what the product, it is so beside the point—that mediocre societal conditions are the inevitable results. But if everyone suspended their participation in this peculiar game of expressive politics and acted more normally, then, given that this is a systemic problem, the totalitarian system would be fundamentally challenged. This is the site where Goffman's notion of the public meets Arendt's.

The Representation of Self (and Others) and the Public Sphere

Havel is implicitly developing a theme of Goffman's, the interactive constitution of the social order, and this interactive constitution was manifest in the real-life Polish examples from 1968 on. Havel appreciates the fact that in his very peculiar world social interaction pulls in two very different directions: toward and away from the constitution of the totalitarian system. The way people present themselves to each other in everyday life determines the fate of the regime. The state, supported by its ideology and terror, demands interaction according to a prescribed script. Individuals can act together and subvert the authorized script, although they do not just freely choose, and the consequences of their bonded choices can be critical. This is less a question of instrumental purpose than of interactive expression. The shopkeeper is not going to help or hinder the unity of the workers of the world. By putting the sign in his shop window, he presents himself as a loyal subject of the official script. By not putting the sign in the window, he presents himself in an entirely different way. Here we apprehend how Goffman's understanding of public life can contribute to Arendt's understanding, how Goffman can be a guide to the origins of the democratic alternative to totalitarianism.

The interactions of Havel's greengrocer and brewmaster, of the Akademia Ruchu street performers, passersby, and militia officers, and of the National Theater director and actors and their audience, including the officials in the Soviet embassy and the Central Committee of the Polish Communist Party, all involve difficulties and tensions over the "definition of the situation." Goffman in his many works highlights how a working consensus concerning the definition of a situation is necessary for social life. Sometimes his focus is on consensus formation and maintaining social order.[5] Sometimes it is on the self.[6] At times it is on consensus disruption. At other times it is on the work done to overcome disruption.[7] Sometimes he is concerned with how the structural complexities of modernity are worked through so that agreement on definitions of social situations can be sustained.[8] And at other times his focus is on what happens in the unique circumstance when the complexities are simplified through coercion.[9] His viewpoint shifts from the individual's, and his or her project of impression management, to the group's, and its operation as a team in sustaining a working consensus. We observe here how axial change has been sustained in and through the interaction order, through new patterns of presentations of self and teamwork.

In the old regime, everyday interactions drew upon two competing frameworks, an ideological one and a nonideological one. People presented themselves in everyday life according to the ideological framework but with some distance from that framework. The makers of theater (and film, literature, social science, etc.) and the censors faced each other utilizing the competing frameworks. Regime opponents tried to assert a new working definition of the situation. Moving the prevailing definition, of course, was not as easy as putting or not putting a Workers of the World Unite sign in a shop window. As Goffman observes: "A 'definition of a situation' is almost always to be found, but those who are in the situation ordinarily do not create this definition, all they do is to assess correctly what the situation ought to be for them and then act accordingly."[10]

The project of the opposition to the prevailing everyday order was to detach the nonideological from the ideological. Role distancing was required, crucial to gaming with the censor and writing and reading between the lines. Recall the actions of the director and the militia official in the street-theater performances of Akademia Ruchu. The project developed, moving from the attempt to breathe life into the existing balance between the ideological and the nonideological, to the attempt to secede from the world of official ideological definition.

The tension between the ideological rendition of social action and action independent of such definition was always there. What changed was how the tension was expressed. At the worst of times, independence could only be expressed through dutiful use of official language and prescribed cultural forms, utilizing role distance and cultural ambiguity. In better times, the official script could be artfully amended and then applied. Thus, socialist humanism and Marxism with a human face were ways to introduce liberal ideals into the socialist order. At the times of systemic challenge, though, such ideological games were abandoned and the more fundamental work of secession from the ideological order proceeded.

In a student cabaret in Warsaw in 1955, the first of the alternative youth theaters in Poland presented its work. In the basements of university dorms and in cultural houses, students read to other students the slogans of the regime. With the simple movement of an eyebrow, the recited ideological clichés became their opposites. Criticism was in fact possible even without the eyebrow. The context and expectations of the audience together worked to illuminate the absurdity of official texts, and the sociality of theater made for the shared recognition of the absurdity.

Something different occurred during the events of 1968. The year started with the controversies over the production of *Dziady*. The play's direct political message, from our point of view, was not its most critical significance. As politics, it was just an elaboration of the sort of work done by the alternative youth theaters, a mild tweaking of the powers, expanding upon the official notion of a "Polish Road to Socialism." That post-Stalinist innovation had entailed the authorities' promotion of Polish romantic literature in schools, in film, and in theater. The National Theater added a little anti-Soviet element to this, whether intentionally or unintentionally. They took official ideology and applied it to their purposes. The nationalist challengers within the party did a similar thing, focusing on anti-Semitism instead of anti-Sovietism. This was a conflict among ideological interpretations, among competing attempts to capture official truth. The student demonstrations, in and beyond the theater, as long as they were centered on this conflict, as long as they were represented using the official language, its newspeak, were more of the same. But viewed from the interactive perspective, considering the face-to-face constitution of public life, something else was emerging. While the claim being made was for a liberal socialist university, using the official rhetoric, the order was not challenged. But then students started to talk and interact with each other on a more straightforward grounding. They opposed censorship and favored greater freedom within the universities, and they met with each other, spoke, and acted together on the basis of this commitment, not in order to find a more perfect road to socialism. They abandoned the attempt merely to balance the ideological and nonideological frames. The commitment to a humane Marxism and a liberal communism now seemed fruitless. Instead their commitment was to independent interaction, to a nonideological presentation of self.

This shift, from playing with the balance between the official and the unofficial to constituting a nonideological alternative, started slowly in the 1970s and in subsequent years came to dominate independent practices. In some ways the everyday became the model for the public; in our understanding, the public in Goffman's sense was utilized as the model for the public in Arendt's. This secession of the nonideological from the ideological represented to the participants and observers of the action a new public order.

Sustaining that secession was no easy matter. People met and acted together, defining and defending freedom by constituting definitions of social situations in which the nonideological and ideological frames were related in ways that ran counter to the existing order. A new way of interacting was introduced in the 1968 theater performance. In the same fashion, but on a much larger scale, the 1980s strikes at the Gdansk shipyards sustained a free public life by enacting changed relations in public. When a democratic opposition developed in the 1970s in Poland, crucial to its definition was that its participants published their names and addresses in their illegal publications. In the words of the most articulate leader of this movement, "they acted as if they lived in a free society," and a free society resulted. They presented themselves to each other as independent citizens and in the process they created an independent public.[11]

The new social order was public in the senses both of Arendt and of Goffman. Solidarity, the great union and social movement, became well known. If we think about axial changes of our recent past, it played a central role. The heroic Lech Walesa was on center stage, a fact recognized by his winning the Nobel Peace Prize. Although he was one of the people to play a central role, his heroism was built upon everyday practices that persisted through time and have been too often overlooked. A very special framing and definition of the situation was involved, a definition of the situation that Arendt called a lost treasure of the revolutionary tradition.

Appearing in Truth

The authorities of the old bloc tried to maintain an ideological definition of the situation. They conflated knowledge and power, presenting an official truth and demanding that people appear to follow its edicts. The democratic movement from 1968 onward challenged the imposed relationship by presenting alternative appearances. Havel did not wonder what would happen if the greengrocer did not *believe* in the slogan "workers of the world unite" and its relevance to his shop; that was a given. At issue was whether people would *appear* as loyal subjects of the official script. The events of 1968 in Poland began as an official game but pointed in the direction of going beyond official truths and ideologically justified activities. The three snapshots of life after those events revealed how this going beyond became a part of everyday social existence.

When Havel wrote about "living in truth" he was not being a naïve romantic, counseling speaking truth to power in a heroic battle. The truth he promoted is of a much more realistic and mundane sort. It involves the grocer and the brewer acting upon the factual truths of their everyday existence: separating the interpretation of politics from the reality of selling fruits and vegetables and brewing beer. They do this by changing the frame of their actions, by appearing apart from the official truth. They do not oppose the communist authority's ideology with anticommunist ideology. They oppose it by interacting within a framework that does not include ideology. They interact in a way that is true to their vocational commitments.

This distancing from official ideology was achieved, as we have seen, in theaters and beyond starting in 1968, using the expressive techniques of face-to-face interactions. These techniques turned the anti-Russian lines of a nineteenth-century play into a major challenge to the totalized order of previously existing socialism. They made the kitchen tables of that old order into nascent free public domains. They turned many private apartments into a network of independent bookstores, and they turned a few apartments into central public forums.

In each of these settings, the complicated relationship between truth and politics was expressively addressed. The truth of plays, of personal relationships, of poetry and history, was represented, but the interpretation of the official ideology was not challenged by an antiofficial inter-

pretation. Openness to alternative political positions, a principled commitment to alternative interpretations, characterized the politics of opposition. The representation of the openness, the appearance in front of
others, the ability to meet and act in concert, were the interactive elements that anticipated the changes of 1989. They are the small things that
constituted a major geopolitical transformation.

3   **1989: New Definitions of the Situation**

The theoretical implications of the collapse of socialism, the socialism of the Soviet bloc, have yet to be fully assimilated by social, cultural, and political theorists. Usually when we think about the meanings of 1989, we think about big geopolitical issues: the fall of an empire, the victory of capitalism, the end of an ideology, if not ideology in general, the end of history, an international effervescence of democracy, the victory of civil society. These are important matters, properly at the center of our attention, as are the issues of the consequences of the momentous breakthroughs of '89. We consider how the collapse of the Soviet bloc, and the Soviet Union after it, have changed just about everything in our geopolitical landscape. We wonder whether it is fruitful any longer to think about a systematic alternative to capitalism, even when we realize the need for alternative ways of doing things. We consider the changing relationship between force and reason and sensation, and have a sense that a magical type of political thought (ideology) is, or at least ought to be, a thing of the past. We study the various transitions to democracy and consider appropriate models of democratic constitution, institutional design, and market consolidation. We appreciate how voluntary associations, social movements, and a free public life opened up the possibilities for these transitions and how they continue to support them.

Yet the theoretical implications of the global changes in our recent past go beyond these large-scale transformations and geopolitical challenges. It is in the microstructures of social interaction that the innovations of political culture become apparent, as these innovations, in their interactive contexts, constitute public space. These microstructures, I suggest, form the foundation of democratic culture. This foundation was, as we have seen, initiated in 1968. It began supporting new democratic structures in 1989. In this chapter, we examine how that support worked.

The Definition of the Situation

There was a dramatic moment in 1989 when the dynamic of a new definition of the situation became strikingly apparent. On December 17 of that year, the security forces of Romania's Ceausescu regime attacked protestors in the city of Timisoara.[1] There, the parishioners of a Hungarian pastor, Laszlo Tokes, were attempting to prevent his arrest, and their Romanian neighbors, including many students, were demonstrating in their defense. In the manner typical of the repressive regime, the police fired on the crowd, resulting in a massacre. Despite these events, Nicolae Ceausescu left the country on a state visit to Iran, apparently confident that the radical changes occurring throughout the Soviet bloc would not effect his hold on power. At that time neither the circle immediately surrounding the communist dictator nor the general populace imagined that the old order was threatened by these events. In previous years, social protests, particularly strikes, had occurred in Romania, and repression had been effective. After the fact, it is easy to see that the geopolitical situation had changed and that the old way of doing things in Romania, as in Czechoslovakia, Poland, East Germany, and elsewhere, was over. But it was not so clear at the time.

Our problem is to understand how it became clear, and this is where the definition of the situation comes in. When Ceausescu returned from Iran, he called for a state-managed mass demonstration in support of the prevailing order. But something strange happened. It became apparent during the televised rally that the definition of the situation had changed. When the dictator began speaking to the vast assembled gathering, people booed, first in the back of the crowd and then more generally. Pro-government chants were slightly modified to become chants of derision. Totalitarian unity was disrupted. Ceausescu had to retreat rapidly from the disordered scene. There was an open revolt and the means of repression were no longer up to the task. In the crowd, as people interacted with one another, a demonstration that was meant to bestow legitimacy on the regime very rapidly withdrew it. The authority of the dictator could visibly be observed to be melting away.

In the days that followed, a war between repressive forces ensued. Apparently the Securitate, fighting for the old order, battled against the army, which aligned itself with an emerging authority made up of former communist leaders, onetime associates of Ceausescu who were then out of favor. After the fact, there has been much suspicion about the actual identity of the new authorities and the meaning of the transformation they ushered in. For our purposes, what is crucial is that the changes were supported by mass mobilizations. These constituted and were fortified by a new, shared definition of the situation: the old regime came to be seen as mortal, and radical political change now seemed possible. People who would not have dared talk to each other openly before now did, and they acted in concert in entirely new ways. Although what was then perceived as revolutionary change may now appear to have been an attempt to preserve much of the old communist order, it is significant that for this to have occurred change had to be defined as revolutionary by the people on the streets. Ultimately, this definition had its own momentum.

I want to be clear. I am not suggesting that it was always possible to "just say no" to the regime. I am not arguing that there were no extra-situational factors that made it possible to turn an exercise in legitimizing a totalitarian dictator into a mass revolt. What I am arguing is that in order for the structural conditions to lead to change, a shared change in the definition of the situation had to become public and had to be acted upon. Large groups of people, acting and interacting in concert and contrary to the restrictions of the regime, constituted a transforming political power.

That this was happening became clear thanks to the fact that the actions and interactions were broadcast on television. The central place of television in the Romanian revolt was noted immediately.[2] The most heated battles between the new powers and the defenders of the old order occurred around the television station. The end of the old order was defined in the interactions on the streets, but the interactions were extended throughout the nation through televised broadcasts, which rendered the changes real in their consequences.

There were, however, important limits to the changes, which were most apparent in their infamous climax: the trial and execution of Ceau-

sescu and his wife, Elena. First, on December 26, 1989, there was a brief
announcement: an "extraordinary military court" had tried Ceausescu
and his wife. A few hours later (at 1:30 a.m.), the television showed its first
footage of the trial and announced the verdict: "The sentence was death
and the sentence was executed." The verdict was proclaimed in the name
of the "Council of National Salvation," a then faceless executive body.
Throughout that day, the videotape of the trial and the executed leader's
body were repeatedly shown on television. A new political situation was
being defined in this broadcast, but what form that situation would take
was quite unclear.

In comparison with the momentous changes in Poland, Hungary, and
Czechoslovakia earlier in 1989, the way the changes unfolded in Romania
is disturbing. Interactions contributing to the definition to the situation
there were marked by authoritarian negation instead of democratic affir-
mation. The booing at the mass rally expressed a simple negation. The
"no" was directed to the dictator, although the grounds for the political
judgment remained unarticulated, hence unclear. Without an articulated
judgment, there could be no living in truth in the sense of Havel. The opposite of a lie is not necessarily the truth. The opposition to dictatorship
does not necessarily lead to democracy. A Foucaultian detachment from
a truth regime need not imply an Arendtian distancing of truth from politics. These simple propositions were dramatically revealed by the later
course of events in Romania.

We can point to all sorts of structural explanations why things worked
out so roughly in Romania. The dictatorship was particularly repressive,
the economy particularly devastated, the opposition particularly full of
shady characters. In the interactions of the popular demonstrators, these
structural factors found their expression as limitations on their definitions of the situation. They could only articulate and show among themselves an opposition to a brutal form of modern tyranny, totalitarianism.
They were not able to marshal the power of politics in the service of democratic purposes in a sustained and differentiated fashion.

This is not to belittle the importance of the Romanian events of December 1989. I am here pointing to something that is both obvious and
overlooked. Theoretically, I am underscoring the need to synthesize the
insights of the interactive sociology of Erving Goffman with the political
theory of Hannah Arendt. The synthesis illuminates some of the special
legacies of 1989, particularly as they are revealed in different sets of circumstances, in the political experiences of Czechoslovakia and Poland
and that of Romania.

The Social Definition of Power and Freedom:
Czechoslovakia and Poland

It may be obvious that the transformation in Romania was not likely to follow the same path as those in Czechoslovakia or Poland, but why was this so situationally? What occurred in the moment of transformation that led to such different outcomes? Answering these questions requires a close consideration of the way the definition of the new situation is formed. In Czechoslovakia and Poland, the new definition went beyond the act of simple negation of totalitarianism. There were a number of distinctly different definers with distinctly different voices, and these voices and their power of definition had histories. In these countries there were interactively constituted alternative publics, something strikingly absent in Romania. The definitions of the situations there were built upon shared and sustained cultural, political, and social experiences.

: : :

Although the events leading to the changes of '89 in Czechoslovakia were fast and dramatic, they had a social background.[3] The Charter 77 movement and VONS, the Committee for the Defense of the Unjustly Persecuted had sustained an alternative at the margins of political life for over a decade, coordinating oppositionist seminars, vibrant political debate, and theoretical discussions. There had also been significant Catholic Church–based social mobilizations developing apart from the officially sanctioned political order starting in 1985, when 150,000 Czechs and Slovaks marked the eleven hundredth anniversary of the death of Saint Methodius. In the oppositional activities of Charter 77 and VONS, sophisticated alternatives to the regime's imposed order were discussed; in the Catholic activity, a fairly broad segment of the population had experienced a public life set apart from the regime. Yet the oppositional world of such figures as Vaclav Havel, Rita Klimova, Jan Carnogursky, Petr Pithart, and Pavel Bratinka was cut off from the general population, and the Catholic movement, ultimately, was focused on the concerns of only a small segment of believers, a group that cannot be identified with the whole nation (as at least some maintain is the case in Poland).

But in 1989 this isolation and segmentation of public participation came to an end. Students organized themselves. Discussion groups worked on the border between the official and the oppositional, and the spread of samizdat readership prepared the ground for a direct challenge to the previously existing order. A demonstration called by the officially supported youth organization for November 17, to mark the fiftieth anniversary of the martyrdom of Jan Opletal, a Czech student murdered by the Nazis, took an antiregime turn. After meeting at a cemetery, a larger than officially anticipated group turned the commemoration of past sufferings into a demonstration against the present communist order. The assembly left the cemetery and marched to Wenceslas Square, the setting of great moments in twentieth-century Czechoslovak politics, in 1918, 1948, and 1968. They called for freedom and change and were met by brutal repression from riot police. Soon after, a strike was called, which spread quickly from the students of Charles University to students around the country, then to actors and other people in theater, to oppositional circles, and eventually to industrial workers. Three days after the initial demonstration, diverse elements of Czech society came together to form the Civic Forum—the students and actors who were engaged in the initial protests, members of Charter 77, VONS, the Movement for Civic Freedoms, and Rebirth (the club of excommunicated communists), as well as individuals from puppet parties of the regime. The way they defined the situation with each other, through heated discussions and agreements on common action, and the way they interacted with the regime, shaped the course of transformational events in Czechoslovakia.

Beyond an analysis of the formation of Civic Forum and the twists and turns of its negotiations with the party state, we should pay special attention to what went into the definition of the situation, how the definition of the transformational situation in Czechoslovakia differed from that in Romania. Although for a long time, both the Czechoslovak and the Romanian regimes had been extremely repressive, in striking contrast to the Polish and Hungarian regimes, the events of 1989 were very different. Some of the difference has to do with how the regimes themselves acted, no doubt, but even more important is how the oppositional definition of the situation differed in the two cases. In Romania, the first mass mobilization was capable of saying no, but the agency of the address was secret and unclear and ultimately the language of address was violence. In Czechoslovakia, the "no" was articulated by the Civic Forum, a differentiated body made up of different actors, former communists and anticommunists, those who still had dreams about socialism with a human face as well as those who opposed all isms, veterans of the opposition alongside young students. All these groups were held together through the leadership of Vaclav Havel, a remarkable political figure clearly identified as a democratic hero. Under his leadership, a free interactive public was formed.

There was humor and romance in the Magic Lantern, the Prague theater where the opposition debated and formulated its politics. The key oppositional actors had conducted themselves in widely varied ways during communist rule and continued to differ among themselves after. But they were able to act in concert in their negotiations with the authorities, without losing their distinct identities. They were able to sustain a democratic definition of the situation. They defined their situation as one of democratic transformation, and as their interactions were repeated in the streets of Prague and throughout the country, the transformation remained democratic in its consequences.

Havel provided the classic text that can serve as a guide to understanding the dramatic events he also led. In "The Power of the Powerless," as we observed in chapter 2, he tells the tale of a greengrocer who does not put a Workers of the World Unite sign in his shop window.[4] Havel reviews with the reader the meaningless of the sign, but also the immense implications should the grocer take down the sign. Not only would he lose his job. His family would suffer. He would lose friends. His life would be fundamentally overturned. But Havel also considered what would happen if the grocer, in concert with those around him, came to "live in truth." He speculated that their world then would be transformed. Totalitarianism would come to an end. In 1989, life imitated theoretical speculation. Networks of people living in truth, or in Goffman's terms, networks of people constituting transformed social definitions of the situation, politically created a democratic alternative to totalitarianism. Please note that these webs of new definitions of the situation, established by people who had some experience living in truth and by those who were significantly more cautious, meant that there was a capacity to openly contest alternative means of transformation. This capacity developed only later in Romania.

On the other hand, experience in sustaining a free politics had also been rather limited in Czechoslovakia. After 1968 and the repression of the Prague Spring, not only oppositionists, such as Havel, but even liberal communists were subjected to systematic repression. The party state had successfully atomized the society. The world of historic dissent was not visible for average Czech and Slovak citizens. This was in striking contrast to the situation in Poland. There an additional element of the interactive creation of the political can be examined.

: : :

The changes in Poland were developed over a long period of time and had become institutionalized. Opposition intellectuals had developed a highly elaborated alternative cultural system, and the vast majority of the population had links to Solidarity. The sort of "no" articulated in the face of Soviet totalitarianism was a matter of long experience; it had been expressed in 1956, '68, '70, '76, and throughout the 1980s. But much more than negation was involved in those expressions. As in Czechoslovakia alternative positions were represented, but in Poland these alternatives had a history and were systematically and intentionally developed. In Romania, the definition of the situation was unitary. In Czechoslovakia, it was diversified but very much an immediate improvisation. In Poland, a temporal dimension further enriched the democratic quality of the definition. The interactive public did not exist situationally only in space but also through time.

Adam Michnik famously formulated the opposition's central organizing imperative in the late 1970s: to act as if one lived in a free society.[5] Michnik realized that if people acted as if they lived in a free society, they would, in the process, constitute free public space. He drew out the theoretical implications of what was developing in the private spaces of family and friends, which we observed in chapter 1. This strategy spread from a relatively small circle of opposition intellectuals to the broad societal movement of Solidarity, as we observed in chapter 2.

That this simple opposition strategy had immense potential, beyond negation, was revealed during the societal mobilization for the first visit to Poland of Pope John Paul II. In communion with their faith and their compatriot, the Polish pope, the population saw themselves set apart from the communist authorities. They conducted themselves with dignity, and the authorities could do nothing but accept their powerlessness. Some saw in this a true, Catholic Poland. For others the lesson was less specific, but still they saw a self-organized society, independent of the party state. Definitions of the situation varied, but they had in common the characteristic of freedom.

The struggle against officialdom was a long and hard one in Poland. There was a long history of opposition to the Soviet-imposed order, and this history shaped the political landscape. From the immediate postwar period, through the consolidation of Polish Stalinism, the Polish October of 1956, the events of March 1968 and the strikes of December 1970, 1976, and 1980, and on to the struggles of Solidarity above and below ground, a full spectrum of political orientations and groupings developed in Poland. It was the great accomplishment of Solidarity to incorporate just about all opposition forces in the battle against the party state, and it is no surprise that they quickly separated once the common foe disappeared. Acting as if one lived in a free society created freedom dramatically and symbolically in key public events. The highlights included the papal visits, the nationwide strikes, the signing of accords between the communists and the union, the open actions of an independent workers' movement, and the first relatively free elections to put an end to a totalitarian regime. The self-constituted freedom also involved less visible actions: publishing clandestine newspapers, journals, and books, conducting illegal seminars, unionizing, and—the climax—working out the project of democratic transition through roundtable negotiations. The roundtable was a political form that repeated itself throughout the old bloc and was a key to the new definitions of the situation that emerged, a new political form.[6] But note the special place it played in the Polish transition. It established the conditions for an election, which allowed the general public, as a free public, to democratically choose fundamental political transformation. Acting as if one lived in a free society did in fact bring such a society into being, and not only at the margins.

This points to an additional constitutive element of free politics. The Romanian case reveals the power and limitations of negation. The Czech case shows how linked acts of living in truth can come together to form a self-reflective and strategically capable form of power, up to the task of confronting and prevailing over a totalitarian opponent. In Poland, we observe how coordinated actions based upon the principle of freedom constituted a free public, which was capable of rapid institutionalization.

Relations in Public

My task in this chapter is to highlight how the interactively constituted politics of small things affected the course of postcommunism in three settings, not to make invidious comparisons between transitions to democracy. That the groundwork for free political action was better prepared in 1989 in Poland than in Romania, Czechoslovakia, or for that matter anywhere else in the former Soviet bloc, is obvious, as is the fact that the special advantage this preparation provided has been relatively short lived. There are also benefits that accrue to late developers. Thus, the first free elections in the rest of Eastern and Central Europe were not, for the most part, as limited as the first elections in Poland had been. And the advantages of sustained relatively free public activity in a totalitarian context are easily gained in more liberal circumstances.

Compare, for example, the development of the oppositional free press in Poland with the press in present-day Russia. Despite the fact that the press in Russia today is under very significant pressure, it is still freer than the press ever was in communist Eastern Europe. Poland did have a fairly well developed civil society in the communist period, and this was an advantage in the early postcommunist years, probably key to the success of the radical economic program. The new authorities had legitimacy with the public and utilized this successfully. But such is a story already well told, and it leads to false controversies, in my opinion, having to do with a strategy of transition and the relative importance of economy, state, and civil society.[7]

Rather, what I am trying to accomplish in these overviews of the struggles to constitute a democratic alternative to totalitarianism is a glimpse at the interactive dimensions of the politics of small things: the networked political definition of the situation as an active project of politics. In Romania, we saw the dynamics of the definition of the situation. In Czechoslovakia, we saw how a differentiation by those doing the defining facilitated a democratic antitotalitarian definition. I have turned to the overview of the Polish experience to underscore the importance of the temporal dimension in sustaining a democratic transformation. Experience of political action over time solidifies free democratic action, gives depth, breadth, and diversity to the definitions of the situation. Even more than solidifying definitions it actively creates them. The definitions of the situation add up over time to create a fully constituted free public domain.

Small Things in a Great Transformation

On the streets of Bucharest, Prague, and Warsaw, people constituted space for themselves to act freely. Crucial to their actions is what I am calling here the politics of small things. But their capacity to act freely was differently constrained, and the outcomes of their free action were quite different. The differences illuminate the theoretical advantage of Arendt's position, versus Foucault's, on political culture. On the streets of the three cities, action was detached from the truth regime of previously existing socialism—in this regard participants in the opposition did not differ. They did differ, however, in how they related truth with politics. In Romania, the relationship was still very intimate, as was manifested in the trial of the dictator and his wife. In Czechoslovakia, an improvised plurality separated the new political force from interpretation and grounded it in the factual. In Poland, the interactive public was already institutionalized, with an ongoing history of searches for factual truth and competition over interpretations of the events at hand. Political pluralism was the new challenge.

Does this prove that in the final analysis civil society and not the power of the state or the economy has been the key to axial change in our recent past? I want to be clear. This is not my argument. I just want to state that the politics of small things, often summarized in the notion of the importance of civil society, provided an important, if somewhat elusive, base of power, not that it is the ultimate source of power. This more minimal argument should be kept in mind as we try to understand our contemporary difficulties. The politics of small things is not as apparent a source of power as the power of the economy and of the state, but it is there. The events it comprises are not as televisual as suicide bombings and military actions. Yet the presence and the elusiveness of the politics of small things help clarify some of the major problems we confront in the war on terrorism in the aftermath of the attacks of September 11, 2001. The politics of small things broadens the political landscape in a way that is not often recognized. Its importance in the transformations of 1989 gives the lie to the notion that terrorism is the only tactic available to the powerless, and stands as a cautionary lesson for those who imagine that the war on terrorism must necessarily or primarily involve military hardware.

In the next chapters, I will try to substantiate these assertions. But before I do, we need to appreciate what happened in the great transformation of Eastern and Central Europe from the point of view of our theoretically informed understanding of the politics of small things. I have been suggesting that a great transformation occurred between 1968 and 1989, and I have highlighted what might be termed the micro-origins of post-totalitarianism. We have observed three key elements: "living in truth," the extension of the kitchen table, and the formation of publics.

"Living in truth." The most radical break in the formation of the political culture of previously existing socialism occurred in 1968, not in the land where "Marxist humanism" and "socialism with a human face" were tried and defeated by Soviet tanks, i.e., Czechoslovakia, but in Poland. There the liberalization was short-circuited, but, in the terms of Havel's essay, a politics built upon the notion of living in truth was initiated. Key was the fact that those who were concerned with issues of freedom and justice stopped using the official language to pursue their goals. They took down the Workers of the World Unite sign from their interactive windows and pursued humanism and politics with a human face without justifying their claims using the regime's newspeak. They pursued their political principles not by attacking one ideology, communism, with another, anticommunism, but by withdrawing from ideological discourses, that is, discourses that presented interpretations as truths and which were so committed to their interpretations as to substitute opinion for fact.

The extension of the kitchen table. Such distancing from the demands of the previously existing socialist regimes was, as we have seen, built into normal, everyday life around kitchen tables. People began there to work not only at presenting themselves in everyday life truthfully, but also at constituting an interactive space that opened up this activity in different and broader contexts. In Poland and Czechoslovakia, but not in Romania, there were networks of people issuing alternative publications, meeting in small seminars, discussing forbidden facts and interpretations. I have emphasized here not the substance of this work but the significance of the performances that helped establish the places.

Formation of publics. Alternative publics were formed in these performances, as we observed in considering the snapshots in chapter 1, and these publics had great political significance. Even where these spaces were restricted to small circles, as in Czechoslovakia, they played, at the moment of systemic transformation, a key role in yielding peaceful and unambiguous change. The absence of such public space contributed, as we have also seen, to the violence and uncertainty of change in Romania. But where the alternatives were more extensive and had developed over a longer period of time, they played a major role in the transformation and became a resource for democratic consolidation. This was the case in Poland.

In fact, there was a sense in which the institutionalized network of public life in Poland and the more improvised network in Czechoslovakia were not alternative publics but the *only* publics in those societies during the socialist period and its immediate aftermath. Arendt tells the story of totalitarianism as one in which pubic life is destroyed. A definitive characteristic of a totalitarian order is the absence of a public realm. There was no place in totalitarian imagination and practice for people to speak and act in the presence of others as equal and free agents, to establish a place in which to act independently and in concert, to create political power in the Arendtian sense. That people did still have this capacity and could create what Goffman calls the underlife of a total institution became manifest around the kitchen table. The great transformation was very much shaped by the extension of such public capacity.

Looking toward the New Century

Some might argue that the story just told of living in truth, of the power of the powerless, of the politics of small things, pertains only to the opposition to late-twentieth-century oppressions, things of the past. There was something special about the democratic opposition to communism in its last decades that marked the democratic transition, a special invention addressed to a historically specific situation. Clearly there is a moral dimension to the story that is inspiring, a dimension that made Vaclav Havel, the president of a small and marginal country, into a significant world leader. But how it is linked to our times is not at all clear. Although I was able to make the link in my examination of cynicism in the United States and of the question of the intellectual in democratic society, there is still a sense that that was then and this is now.[8] We live in times of globalization and neoliberalism, terror and antiterror, a time when new military threats seem most pressing. Stories of people learning around kitchen tables to define the contours of their immediate political life may appear little more than quaint. That I made the connection was a matter of personal biography, of specific work in comparative historical sociology, not necessarily of its general applicability to political invention or political experience.

Yet as we observe radical critics of the prevailing global order turn to terror, and as we observe the military response of the hegemonic power, the United States—punishing all who disagree, declaring that if you're not with us you're against us—it seems to me that an appreciation of the politics of small things is just what we are missing, across the political spectrum. We have discussed the emergence in 1968 of the politics of small things as a potent force, a force that developed and contributed to the momentous changes of 1989. We now turn to the politics of small things as it provides a critical perspective on the great challenges of the new century and as it presents alternatives to the stark contrasts of civilizational confrontations, jihads, wars on terrorism, and battles against globalization. The politics of small things, we will see, can emerge from a serious close reflection upon the events of September 11, 2001. Alternatives will be examined in the following chapters.

We will consider how the key actors on various sides of the war on terrorism differently explain the end of the twentieth century and the major traumatic events of our recent past, and how they confront each other in terms of different theories of power. By looking closely at the meaning of the events of September 11, 2001, we will observe the grand narratives and theories of history embraced by the terrorists, the antiterrorists and the anti-antiterrorists. By considering the bridge between the twentieth and twenty-first centuries, constructed of wars, grand narratives, and more delimited human actions, we will observe the ways in which less grand stories and actions present alternatives.

4

2001: Narratives in Conflict

The twenty-first century began on a beautiful autumnal morning in New York City. Before 9/11, the nineteenth century looked long, from the French Revolution to World War I; the twentieth short, from the Russian Revolution through Soviet and Nazi totalitarianism to the fall of communism, and the twenty-first—the post–cold war era and globalization—anticlimactic.[1] Since 9/11, the twentieth century does not look as short as it once did, and the world is now defined by the threat of global terror and the struggle against it.

September 11, 2001: the facts are well known. They were observed simultaneously worldwide through the globalized media. People in India, South Africa, Egypt, and the United States watched the events as they happened. Interpretations of the facts are, however, contested. Their outcome too remains unclear, dependent on interpretations both of the facts of the attacks and of the actions based on those facts. The configuration of these facts, interpretations, conflicts, and understandings represents a fundamental change in historical imagination.

A distanced perspective is not yet available. As I write this, much has still to be determined about the resulting changes in the global political order. But already some things are becoming apparent: Old cold war antagonisms are buried. Regional conflicts and tensions, from Kashmir to Gaza, have been globalized. The secularization thesis seems to be wildly mistaken. Religion is ascendant as a guide to political actions, both democratic and profoundly antidemocratic, and the sacralization of the totalitarian temptation has become a vivid part of the political repertoire.[2] The targeting of civilians as an aim of military action has reached its extreme conclusion. "Collateral damage" is, without any ambiguity, the goal of this terrorism, whereas in Vietnam and Hiroshima there was at least some ambiguity. Rhetorically a "war on terrorism" has been declared, and bombs have been dropped and troops deployed. But confusion still surrounds these actions. It is quite uncertain what brought about our present predicaments and how we can overcome them.

Thinking with reference to the emergent periodization can be helpful. How is the new century connected to the longer twentieth century? What theories of power underlie different theories of connection held by the conflicting powers? How are the new totalitarian temptations connected to the totalitarian classics and their opponents? There are competing big answers and telling small ones: the big answers of the terrorists, antiterrorists, and anti-antiterrorists but also smaller perspectives and alternatives.

The Sacralized Totalitarian Temptation: The Terrorist Narrative

Soon after the 9/11 attacks, a debate ensued: What is the relationship between terrorism and Islam? There is an official position, shared by most of its critics, which President George W. Bush summarized in remarks at the Islamic Center of Washington, D.C.: "These acts of violence against innocents violate the fundamental tenets of the Islamic faith. . . . The face of terror is not the true faith of Islam. This is not what Islam is all about. Islam is peace. These terrorists don't represent peace. They represent evil and war."[3] College students who opposed the war in Afghanistan nonetheless echoed the official position: "Islam is not the problem," they argued; "war is not the solution."

Yet despite this normative consensus, there is a problem: The 9/11 attackers were all Muslims. Further, terrorism justified by Islamic rhetoric is a worldwide phenomenon, reaching from Palestine to Kashmir, to the Philippines and Indonesia, to northern and southern Africa. Italian prime minister Silvio Berlusconi, observing these phenomena, concluded that Western civilization is superior to that of Islam: "We should be confident of the superiority of our civilization, which consists of a value system that has given people widespread prosperity and guarantees respect for human rights and religion. This respect certainly does not exist in Islamic countries."[4] His statement was widely condemned, and he later backed off from its provocative implications. After all, the worst horrors of the modern age, from anti-Semitism to imperialism to totalitarianism, were Western inventions. The claim of moral superiority is dubious.

Yet, the link between Islam and recent acts of terrorism remains. Salman Rushdie observes the difficult situation:

> "This isn't about Islam." The world's leaders have been repeating this mantra for weeks, partly in virtuous hope of deterring reprisal attacks on innocent Muslims living in the West, partly because if the United States is to maintain its coalition against terror it can't afford to suggest that Islam and terrorism are in any way related.
>
> The trouble with this necessary disclaimer is that it isn't true. If this isn't about Islam, why the worldwide Muslim demonstrations in support of Osama bin Laden and Al Qaeda? Why did those 10,000 men armed with swords and axes mass on the Pakistan-Afghanistan frontier, answering some mullah's call for jihad? Why are the war's first British casualties three Muslim men who died fighting on the Taliban side?
>
> Why the routine anti-Semitism of the much-repeated Islamic slander that 'the Jews' arranged the hits on the World Trade Center and the Pentagon, with the oddly self-deprecating explanation offered by the Taliban leadership, among others, that Muslims could not have the technological know-how or pull off such a feat?[5]

Confronting the relationship between terrorism and Islam is a difficult task. Simple mistakes must be avoided. The fact that Islam provides the ideological basis for contemporary terrorism in many corners of the globe does not mean that all Muslims are somehow implicated or responsible for the terror. It is clearly a small minority of Muslims that were actively involved in or even supportive of the terrorist attacks on the World Trade Center and the Pentagon. Sympathy may have been more widespread when terror was directed against other targets, generally in the Middle East and most commonly Israel, but also in such hotspots as Kashmir, where terror used by Muslims in the conflict with India and condoned by Pakistan has been common enough. These uses of terrorism, though, do not much differ from its use by Basque and Corsican separatists, the Irish Republican Army, and many other political movements. Terrorism has been a weapon throughout the modern world—there is no Islamic monopoly. Yet there does seem to be something different now.

With his signature polemical vigor, Christopher Hitchens highlights the crucial difference:

> To the Wahhabi-indoctrinated sectarians of Al Qaeda, only the purest and most fanatical are worthy of consideration. The teachings and published proclamations of this cult have initiated us to the idea that the tolerant, the open-minded, the apostate or the followers of different branches of The Faith are fit only for slaughter and contempt. And that's before Christians and Jews, let alone atheists and secularists, have even been factored in. As before, the deed announces and exposes its "root cause." The grievance and animosity predate even the Balfour Declaration, let alone the occupation of the West Bank. They predate the creation of Iraq as a state. The gates of Vienna would have had to fall to the Ottoman jihad before any balm could begin to be applied to these psychic wounds. And this is precisely, now, our problem. The Taliban and its surrogates are not content to immiserate their own societies in beggary and serfdom. They are condemned, and they deludedly believe that they are commanded, to spread the contagion and to visit hell upon the unrighteous. The very first step that we must take, therefore, is the acquisition of enough self-respect and self-confidence to say that we have met an enemy and that he is not us, but someone else. Someone with whom coexistence is, fortunately I think, not possible. (I say "fortunately" because I am also convinced that such coexistence is not desirable).[6]

Hitchens then defines the enemy as "Islamic Fascism." He uses this term because the "deed announces . . . its 'root cause,'" because the violent act is a distinctive form of communication. Hitchens writes as a distinguished man of the left and is reticent to include Soviet communism under the "fascist" heading. Yet what we see in bin Ladenism is a totalitarian mentality. In the totalitarian orders of the twentieth century, both fascist and communist, force defined reason. Truth and power were conflated. Keeping in mind Arendt's consideration of politics and truth, in contrast with Foucault's notion of knowledge and power, there is something special about this type of official truth, based upon a simple idea, which explains the connection between past, present, and future. Terror enforces the official truth. This same configuration, as Hitchens demonstrates in his polemics in the *Nation* and elsewhere, is again part of the political scene. There are, though, significant new elements to this totalitarian scheme.

Bin Laden understands the attraction of power: "When people see a strong horse and a weak horse," he said in a video made shortly after 9/11, "by nature, they will like the strong horse." And he invests violence with magical power:

> Those young men [inaudible] said in deeds, in New York and Washington—speeches that overshadowed all other speeches made everywhere else in the world. The speeches are understood by both Arabs and non-Arabs, even by Chinese. It is above all— the media said. Some of them said that in Holland, at one of the centers, the number of people who accepted Islam during the days that followed the operations were more than the people who accepted Islam in the last 11 years. I heard someone on Islamic radio who owns a school in America say: "We don't have time to keep up with the demands of those who are asking about Islamic books to learn about Islam."[7]

His commitment to the communicative power of violence is coupled with a complete theory of history, deduced from a simple idea. He explains the terrorist jihad against the United States thus:

> We declared jihad against the U.S. government because the U.S. government committed acts that are extremely unjust, hideous, and criminal whether directly or though its support of the Israeli occupation of [Palestine]. . . . This U.S. government abandoned humanitarian feelings by these hideous crimes. It transgressed all bounds and behaved in a way not witnessed before by any power or any imperialist power in the world. Due to its subordination to the Jews, the arrogance and haughtiness of the U.S. regime has reached to the extent that they occupied [Arabia]. For this and other acts of aggression and injustice, we have declared jihad against the U.S., because in our religion it is our duty to make jihad so that God's word is the one exalted to the heights and so that we drive the Americans away from all Muslim countries.[8]

An evil power, the United States, is manipulated by an evil agent, the Jews. In other moments, bin Laden attributes equal demonic force to the crusaders, that is, Christian civilization, presenting a worldview that mirrors Berlusconi's. This creates a political imperative for terrorism, based on religious commitment. The glories of the Islamic past are linked to the glories of its future. The rebirth of the *Khalifa* is insured by the act.

The united community of Muslim believers, the *umna,* will therefore, after the West's overthrow, live under the rule of the law of the prophet
Muhammad.[9] Terrorism thus affirms the religious-political commitment,
confirming the legitimacy of the totalitarian leader. After the 9/11 attacks, an admirer reports to bin Laden: "Hundreds of people used to
doubt you and few only would follow you until this huge event happened.
Now hundreds of people are coming out to join you."[10]

Positively, the appeal and action of bin Ladenism is Islamic, with an
attempt to reenact the glories of the *Khalifa.* Negatively, there is anti-
Americanism, which unites a diverse group of people, with their diverse
concerns, in a commitment to a charismatic leader and his cause. General Pervez Musharaf, the military president of Pakistan, summarizes:

> The Western demonization of OBL, as he is known in Pakistan,
> made him a cult figure among Muslims who resented everything
> from the decline in moral values as conveyed by Hollywood
> movies and TV serials to America's lack of support for the Pales-
> tinians being killed by Israeli occupation forces, to what Russia is
> doing to the Muslims in Chechnya, [to] what the west did to Mus-
> lims in Bosnia and Kosovo, [to] India's oppression of Muslims in
> Kashmir. . . . It is a long list of complaints that has generated a
> strong persecution complex that the OBL cult figure has come to
> embody. He is a hero on the pedestal of Muslim extremism.[11]

In a world of one superpower, anti-Americanism comes easily, and quite
a bit of it is based on reasonable criticism of American deficiencies.[12] In
the case of bin Laden, parts of his totalized hatred of everything American appeals to specific constituencies.

There is, then, a distinctive social structure of ideological and political commitment in the bin Laden organization, quite similar to the social
structure of other twentieth-century movements. Bin Laden declared in
the post–9/11 video:

> The brothers, who conducted the operation, all they knew was
> that they have a martyrdom operation and we asked each of them
> to go to America but they didn't know anything about the oper-
> ation, not even one letter. But they were trained and we did not
> reveal the operation to them until they are there and just before
> they boarded the planes. *[inaudible]* . . . Those who were trained
> to fly didn't know the others. One group of people did not know
> the other group.

The Bush administration, before releasing the tape, publicly suggested that this quote indicated that bin Laden sent unknowing operatives to their deaths in a suicide mission. But this is a misinterpretation, overlooking the more telling structure that bin Laden is celebrating.

Hannah Arendt describes the structure:

> In contradistinction to both tyrannical and authoritarian regimes, the proper image of totalitarian rule and organization seems to me to be the structure of the onion, in whose center, in a kind of empty space, the leader is located; whatever he does—whether he integrates the body politic as in an authoritarian hierarchy, or oppresses his subjects like a tyrant—he does it from within, and not without or above. All the extraordinary manifold parts of the movement . . . are related in such a way that each forms the façade in one direction and the center in the other, that is plays the role of normal outside world for one layer and the role of extremism for another. The great advantage of this system is that the movement provides each of its layers . . . the fiction of a normal world along with a consciousness of being different from and more radical than it. . . . Thus, the sympathizers in the front organizations, whose convictions differ only in intensity from those of party membership, surround the whole movement and provide a deceptive façade of normality to the outside world because of their lack of fanaticism and extremism, while at the same time, they represent the normal world to the totalitarian movement, whose members come to believe that their convictions differ only in degree from those of other people, so that they need never be aware of the abyss which separates their own world from that which actually surrounds it. The onion structure makes the system organizationally shock-proof against the factuality of the real world.[13]

There is more than a strategic "need to know" quality to bin Laden's terrorist network. There is an unusual relation with empirical reality and ideology, institutionalized through a distinctive organizational structure. At the center of the movement are the radical true believers, more moved by the fantastic claims of ideology than by the demands of lived experience. At the periphery of the movement are sympathizers, ordinary people who find the movement's claims appealing but still live a normal existence. In between, there are people who variously blend ideological purity and contact with the concerns of everyday life. In twentieth-century totalitarian movements, the connection between the center and the periphery was accomplished through party and front organizations. The elite of the party was the most attuned to ideology, most remote from the ordinary concerns of daily life. Casual members of front organizations had intimate relations with the concerns of daily life and only remote contact with ideological purity. The front organization and its members convinced outsiders that the new movement had a connection with ordinary concerns, while the party elite convinced them that there was a magical solution to such concerns. Taken together, they transformed political life with something unprecedented. The terrorists' ignorance of the details of their actions is a new manifestation of this totalitarian organizational theme.

In totalitarianism of old the organization articulated the party ideology. There was an official truth, which was modern and scientized. In the new totalitarianism, it is postmodern and sacralized. Its organization appears more fluid, more as a network than as a structure. Instead of hierarchical party structures with front organizations, there are loosely affiliated cells of terror. Alongside these are mosques and schools, which encourage their congregants and students to enlist in the terrorist cause, the jihad. The degree to which these institutions are open in their support varies, and it seems likely that sometimes they are more explicit internally than they are in statements intended for the general public. Along with schools, there are various welfare functions served by religious movements that do not strongly differentiate between caring for the sick and the needy and supporting terror and terrorists.

The Palestinian group Hamas was in fact first a social welfare movement and only later a terrorist organization. Donors, both individual and corporate, contributing to the support of the victims of Israeli occupation and injustice on the West Bank and Gaza may very well not know that their support also goes to the support of suicide bombers. Those supporting Islamic schools in Pakistan, social welfare projects in Kashmir, human rights organizations in Bosnia and Chechnya, may also be supporting activities that they themselves would denounce. The actual suicide bombers on September 11 were ignorant of how their sacrifice fit into the overall plans and message of the jihad. They just knew what their fate was, a promised salvation.

The radical Islamist movement presents itself as being an authentic carrier of the traditional Islam. While I do not have the competence to comment on this on theological grounds, sociologically it is clearly not the case. Even in comparison to relatively recent carriers of the traditional message, they are different. The older generation of Islamic fundamentalists was composed of scholars. The new generation is more often composed of technicians of various sorts.[14] The message is not passed along through theological debate, a sort of Islamic public sphere,[15] but through the sounds and images of the media. The movement is an electronic media manifestation, much more up to date than the totalitarians of the past. In a profile broadcast by CNN on May 12, 1997, bin Laden said, when asked about his future plans, "You'll see them and hear about them in the media. God willing."[16] The electronic media are the stage of the action. How particular acts appear as media events define their political reality.

An al Qaeda recruitment audiotape serves as a substitute for a written manifesto. It says, for example, "These Americans brought . . . Jewish women who can go anywhere in our holy land."[17] The tape passes from hand to hand but is also available on the Internet. This is a global variation on a more rudimentary scheme developed in the struggle against the Shah in Iran and elaborated in the distribution of taped sermons in Egypt and throughout the Muslim world. The preacher addresses his flock through tapes, and their listeners form large constituencies, capable, in Iran, of acting in concert and overthrowing a powerful regime. In the case of anti-American terror, the dramatic act carried out by committed activists, moved by the sermons, is broadcast by global television and radio networks, reaching a broad international audience. A virtual totalitarian organization is produced. Not only the true believers within the terrorist networks (and the religious organizations and schools that support them), but also those who sympathize with the movement's attitudes, are significant. They are the ones who buy T-shirts bearing bin Laden's image on the streets of Jakarta or perfume with his name in Lahore, Pakistan, or Osama bin Laden sweets in Kandahar, Afghanistan.[18] Terrorist networks, instead of hierarchical organizations; religious schools and welfare organizations, instead of party cells and fronts; virtual sympathizers and cultural consumers, instead of party fronts and fellow travelers—this is the social form the totalitarian movement now takes. It is unclear whether such a movement can lead to the establishment of a postmodern totalitarian state. Perhaps the Taliban was one example.

Although this form is different from the social form of the totalitarian movements of the twentieth century, it serves a similar totalitarian purpose, what we sociologists awkwardly name the project of societal dedifferentiation. It is as different as the political manifesto printed on a small press is from video and audiotapes distributed via the Internet and reported by global media corporations. Yet in the last century and this, the task is to impose on a complex society a unified cultural code. In Nazi Germany social life revolved, theoretically, around the science of race, and in the Soviet Union life revolved around class. Through the powers of the party state the theoretical was imposed upon complex realities, yielding repression, censorship, and ideologically driven commands and controls. The same arrangements are to be found in Islamist movements, giving them an appearance of tradition but a reality of modern tyranny. There is a coincidence of traditional and modern forms, a distinctive post-modern configuration. A traditional version of Islam is presented as a means of organizing a modernizing civilization. All that stands in the way of this organization is the work of enemies. When the enemies are over-come, there will be justice.

Differentiation of the state and religion is said to distinguish Christian civilization from Islamic civilization. While Christ and the early Chris-tians were religious oppositionists, accommodating to the political pow-ers, the prophet Muhammad was both a religious and a political leader. The unity of politics and religion has been characteristic of the Ottoman Empire, and of both the Saudi rulers of our day and their major oppo-nent, Osama bin Laden.[19] Yet to assert that contrasting origins lead to essentially and necessarily contrasting histories is to overlook both theo-cratic tendencies in the West and democratic possibilities in Islamic civi-lization.[20] Both anti-Islamic "Orientalists," such as Berlusconi, and Is-lamic totalitarians, such as Bin Laden, make this move.

Bin Laden's response to the fall of the Soviet empire and of modern to-talitarianism more generally in practice reproduces the totalitarian form. He and other Islamist radicals imagine the defeat of the Soviet Union in Afghanistan to have been the prelude to a great Islamic revival. The force of arms is imagined to be a providential force. Religion, politics, and mil-itary struggle are united. The movement is organized like its totalitarian precursors, only now religion, not scientism, is the content, and more contemporary media forms are utilized in the organization. And cen-trally, like the totalitarians of the twentieth century, the Islamic totalitar-ians reveal the truth of their ideology with the force of their terrorism. Christopher Hitchens is right: there is a special affinity with fascism and Nazism. Those movements imagined themselves to be the answer to communism. Liberalism had failed, and communism threatened Western civilization. Now modern liberalism has failed, bringing defeat and im-morality to the Arab and Muslim nations. Communism threatened Is-lamic civilization but was defeated. Now the struggle is being extended to the remaining infidels. This is the account of the longer twentieth century, as it is linked to the twenty-first, that the Bush-Blair official antiterrorist account opposes.

The Official Story: The Antiterrorist Narrative

George W. Bush has outlined the official American position. He presented the central historical thesis in a speech to a joint session of Congress following the 9/11 attacks. The terrorists, he declared,

> are the heirs of all the murderous ideologies of the 20th century. By sacrificing human life to serve their radical visions—by abandoning every value except the will to power—they follow in the path of fascism, and Nazism, and totalitarianism. And they will follow that path all the way, to where it ends: in history's unmarked grave of discarded lies.[21]

Bush, with some diplomatic equivocation, was drawing parallels between the struggles of the twentieth century and those of the twenty-first, and was predicting the same outcome.[22] As America led the struggle and prevailed against communism and Nazism, it will lead the struggle against "terrorism with a global reach," and again it will prevail. In this understanding of history, the United States and its allies are again confronting an evil empire, or at least an evil enemy. Bush on September 11: "Today our nation saw evil, the very worst of human nature."[23]

Tony Blair echoed and amplified Bush's position, pointing to the meaning of subsequent actions:

> This attack is an attack not only on America but on the world, which demands our complete and united condemnation, our determination to bring those responsible to justice and our support for the American people at this time of trial. . . . The world now knows the full evil and capability of international terrorism which menaces the whole of the democratic world. The terrorists responsible have no sense of humanity, of mercy, or of justice. . . . People of all faiths and all democratic persuasions have a common cause: to identify this machinery of terror and to dismantle it as swiftly as possible.[24]

This is the next phase in the global struggle against evil, now appearing as Islamist terror, not to be confused with Islam as a world religion and civilization. It is presented as a struggle for democracy, tolerance, and faith.

Bush is prone to portray the struggle in religious terms. He declared in closing his speech to Congress and the nation: "Freedom and fear, justice and cruelty, have always been at war, and we know that God is not neutral between them."[25] And during his remarks at the National Day of Prayer and Remembrance service on September 14, 2001, in the National Cathedral, he sounded more like a cleric than a political leader when he declared:

> God's signs are not always the ones we look for. We learn in tragedy that his purposes are not always our own. Yet the prayers of private suffering, whether in our homes or in this great cathedral, are known and heard, and understood. . . . As we have been assured, neither death nor life, nor angels nor principalities nor powers, nor things present nor things to come, nor height nor depth, can separate us from God's love. May He bless the souls of the departed. May he comfort our own. And may He always guide our country.[26]

A fight for freedom and democracy and against fanaticism, which is understood as being evil, has replaced the fight for freedom and democracy against atheistic communism. This fight, Bush strongly implies, has divine support.

A righteous political position, supported by the military might of the superpower, constitutes the power of the Bush-Blair position. It reproduces formally the juxtaposition of the cold war era: then it was the free world versus the evil (communist) empire, now it is the free world or the civilized world versus an evil (Islamic) enemy.

Critical Stories

There is much that is problematic about this new crusade.[27] Even those who support the declared "war on terrorism" find problems in the official story. For some, it is a question of tone; this is particularly so for the secular minded. For others, on both the right and the left, there are issues of tactics and strategies.

On the left, Michael Walzer agreed with the notion of a war on terrorism. But his support was premised on a particular understanding of the phrase. If "war" was a metaphor for "struggle, commitment and endurance," Walzer had no problem with the term and with its application. But if it signified grand battles, trench warfare, bombing, and major military campaigns, he had his doubts. In Walzer's view, the war on terrorism should be a "war" involving policing, intelligence, and diplomacy. It should be a war of face-to-face combat, including cloak-and-dagger operations against known terrorists, financial operations against those who would support terrorists, and intellectual struggles that "engage all the arguments and excuses for terrorism and reject them."[28]

There are also strategic and tactical criticisms from the right. While Walzer advocates a metaphoric war, William Kristol has called in no uncertain terms for a literal war. In a series of articles, some coauthored with Robert Kagan, Kristol has opposed diplomacy and multinational coalition building, instead favoring unilateral military action and carefully articulating a nationalist position. He has called for decisive and unconstrained military action and was quick to depict an administration and a president torn by a conflict personified by Secretary of State Colin Powell (Kristol's villain) and Secretary of Defense Donald Rumsfeld (his hero). Soon after the president's address to Congress and the nation, Kristol wrote an editorial entitled "Bush vs. Powell": "Colin Powell wants a war on poverty. The president must go further. Bin Laden is just the first step: the Taliban, Syria and Iraq must each be dealt with in turn. It's no time to go wobbly." When Powell (echoing Tony Blair and many other world leaders) suggested that the attack on the World Trade Center was in fact an attack on the civilized world, Kristol objected. "The president did ask other nations to join us. But he made clear that American honor required first and foremost an American response to this 'wound to our country': 'I will not yield, I will not rest, I will not relent in waging this struggle for freedom and security for the American people.'"[29] Kristol, and other critics on the right, bemoaned the slow unfolding of the war, celebrated the escalation of the conflict, and called for its expansion.[30] They strongly approve of the war but have questioned the vigor with which its goals have been pursued.

These positive criticisms, from the left and the right, do not question the fundamentals of the official story. While they are critical, in differing ways, when it comes to tactics, both accept the necessity of some sort of war on terrorism. And both understand terrorism as a new historic challenge to liberal democracy. Walzer, and the democratic left more generally, view the threat from the perspective of universal values of justice, Kristol, and the democratic right more generally, from a more nationalist perspective. But the two positions differ strikingly in the way they think about the power of the United States as a combatant in the war against terrorism. For those on the right, military power, nationalism, and righteousness are united. For those on the left, each of these dimensions requires caution. The stories they tell appear to be similar but differs in their details, which lead to very different political positions. In this regard, the antiterrorist consensus of the new century parallels the anticommunist consensus of the last century; both entailed significant tensions. Tell the official story with Kristol's emphasis, and the policy pursued will be primarily militaristic and unilateral—the Iraq war is a necessary conclusion. Tell it with Walzer's emphasis, and the policy will be cultural and political, with military options viewed as last resort and then only if pursued in multilateral fashion. Opposition to the war in Iraq follows.

Radical Voices against Antiterrorism: The Antiglobalization Narrative

There have been others, though, who radically question the official historical narrative. While some marginal people joined Osama bin Laden in applauding the attacks on the World Trade Center and the Pentagon as progressive acts, it is hard to find any significant political or intellectual figure in a liberal democracy who did so publicly. Many, however, have viewed the attacks with varying degrees of sympathy and understanding, placing them in an alternative historical narrative. And as the purely or primarily military response to terror prevailed, this sympathy and understanding increased.

A young man in South Africa, Makhaola Ndebele, reported that his first response to the attack was disbelief, but then "this turned to excitement at the enormity of the event. 'America being hit!' Later when I saw how many lives were lost, reality set in, but my excitement was, 'It's finally happening to them,' whereas they thought they were invincible. . . . America got its comeuppance."[31] Such opinion could be heard throughout the world, and often enough in the United States as well. Its expression went beyond feelings, toward analysis and an overall alternative narrative.

At a teach-in on the attacks on the Pentagon and the World Trade Center, Noam Chomsky declared: "The terrorist attacks were major atrocities. In scale they may not reach the level of many others—for example, Clinton's bombing of the Sudan with no credible pretext, destroying half its pharmaceutical supplies and killing unknown numbers of people (no one knows, because the US blocked an inquiry at the UN and no one cares to pursue it). Not to speak of much worse cases, which easily come to mind."[32] While Chomsky is not celebrating or supporting the attacks, by comparing them to an American action in Sudan, which did not provoke major protests, he is placing them within a context that minimizes their enormity and questions the idea that America is a victim of evil forces.

This context was fully portrayed by Arundhati Roy:

The September 11 attacks were a monstrous calling card from a
world gone horribly wrong. The message may have been written
by Bin Laden (who knows?) and delivered by his couriers, but it
could well have been signed by the ghosts of the victims of America's old wars. The millions killed in Korea, Vietnam and Cam-
bodia, the 17,500 killed when Israel—backed by the US—invaded
Lebanon in 1982, the 200,000 Iraqis killed in Operation Desert
Storm, the thousands of Palestinians who have died fighting Israel's occupation of the West Bank. And the millions who died,
in Yugoslavia, Somalia, Haiti, Chile, Nicaragua, El Salvador, the
Dominican Republic, Panama, at the hands of all the terrorists,
dictators and genocidists whom the American government supported, trained, bankrolled and supplied with arms. And this is
far from being a comprehensive list.

She then offered an overview of the present situation:

The desolate landscape of Afghanistan was the burial ground of
Soviet communism and the springboard of a unipolar world dominated by America. It made the space for neocapitalism and corporate globalisation, again dominated by America. And now
Afghanistan is poised to become the graveyard for the unlikely
soldiers who fought and won this war for America.[33]

In a later article she pointed to the political implications:

What freedoms does it [the United States] uphold? Within its
borders, the freedoms of speech, religion, thought; of artistic expression, food habits, sexual preferences (well, to some extent)
and many other exemplary, wonderful things. Outside its borders, the freedom to dominate, humiliate and subjugate—usually
in the service of America's real religion, the "free market". So
when the US government christens a war "Operation Infinite Justice", or "Operation Enduring Freedom", we in the third world
feel more than a tremor of fear.[34]

This is the alternative critical narrative of antiglobalization. The mad-
ness of the attacks of 9/11 is not supported, but it is understood as being
a critical response to globalization and the American empire. The twentieth century saw the triumph of corporate capitalism, serving the interests of the United States, supported by the military might of the United

States. The war on terrorism is but a projection of the globalization project. The United States used Islamists as its fighting surrogate in its struggle against Soviet communism. The surrogates have since become troublesome, so the United States is amassing the coalition against terrorism for a cleanup operation, to maintain its position as the sole remaining superpower.

Alternatives?

The terrorist, antiterrorist, and anti-antiterrorist each assume a theory of history and a theory of historical transformation and power. The terrorists themselves constitute power in a typical totalitarian fashion. Force and reason, terror and ideology, are conflated. They understand their power as it was revealed in Afghanistan, where their military force played a key role in the defeat of the Red Army, leading to the fall of the Soviet Union. They saw in this force a kind of divine will, which they now act upon. The Bush administration views the defeat of communism in a different way. It was the great American cold war victory against the evil empire. Freedom, combined with military force and economic might, prevailed. Now against another evil enemy, global terrorism, the combination will prevail again. Statements by the antiterrorists, under the leadership of George W. Bush, sometimes echo the totalitarian conflation of the terrorists, especially in the assertion that god is on our side. Such resemblance to the enemy recalls the resemblance of communism and anticommunism, fascism and antifascism in the past century. This was most striking in the clash between Nazism, a radical form of anticommunism, and communism, a radical form of antifascism, as François Furet has highlighted.[35]

Critics of globalization oppose both the terrorist and the antiterrorist conflations, but they seem primarily to address the position of the antiterrorists. Central to their case is a questioning of the cold war victory, or at least its value. They reveal the lie of the ideological exaggerations and tell a story that views the past victories of both Islamists and cold warriors as secondary to the ascendance of globalization. They are quiet about the threat of terror today and pay little attention to the significance of totalitarianism in our recent past.

The terrorists, the antiterrorists, and the forces opposing globalization tell big stories. They understand the 9/11 attacks by organizing past and future around their main concerns, with a broad historical sweep. Overlooked is the important part that the politics of small things has played in our recent past, which we have already observed in the cases of the pivotal years of 1968 and 1989.

While those supporting the war on terrorism see the 9/11 attacks as being directed against liberty and democratic ideals, the anti-antiterrorists see the attacks as a response to American hegemonic policies. Thus Howard Zinn counseled: "We need to think about the resentment all over the world felt by people who have been the victims of American military action—in Vietnam, in Latin America, in Iraq."[36]

Zinn's turn to the human level has much to recommend it, even if it is not clear how the cited victims are connected to terrorist acts. One of Arundhati Roy's critics made an interesting suggestion in arguing against her contention that the motivations of the particular terrorists will be forever unknown and against her assertion of the importance of the generalized anger of the victims of American domination as an explanation for the attacks of 9/11. Dennis Brown, a professor at the University of Hertfordshire in England, quotes documents discovered among the belongings of one of the attackers—"I pray to you God to forgive me all my sins, to allow me to glorify you in every possible way"—and offers this commentary: "A hideous blasphemy of prayer before the holocaust of thousands of souls of all faiths. The anti-deity of the hijackers is a god of very small minds. Roy should stick to writing about the small things she knows about."[37] Brown, apparently, means to put Roy in her place. But, it seems to me, there is more to his suggestion than he intended. He suggests the importance of small things in the age of terrorism.

Small Things versus Grand Narratives

In her novel *The God of Small Things*, Arundhati Roy presents a world of infinite complexity in intimate human relationships. The story is set in Kerala in southern India, not far from what has become the central stage of the war against terrorism. The caste system, the Marxist political project, the legacies of colonialism, the superficialities of mass culture, racism, patriarchy, and many other big topics are rendered meaningful by way of their small manifestations. Roy makes the link between past and present problematic, and her characters are depicted with moral ambiguity, save one. The "God of Small Things" is a heroic character, an untouchable, who masters details but is subject to a tragic fate. Vellya Paapen, his father, "feared for his younger son. He couldn't say what it was that frightened him. It was nothing that he had said. Or done. It was not *what* he had said, but the *way* he had said it. Not *what* he did, but the *way* he did it. Perhaps it was just a lack of hesitation. An unwarranted assurance. In the way he walked. The way he held his head."[38] In his very bearing and demeanor, the God of Small Things is a walking affront to injustice. He becomes a master carpenter and a supervisor. He is a political activist and the illicit lover of a woman above his station. His actions transgress the boundaries of the acceptable, but it is his being that stands as the basic challenge and that is the source of joy in a joyless world.

About the illicit lovers, Roy writes: "Instinctively they stuck to the small things. The Big Things ever lurked inside. They knew that there was nowhere for them to go. They had nothing. No future. So they stuck to the small things."[39] Roy's is an elegant, highly textured novel. It does not answer questions but raises them (as Milan Kundera would emphasize).[40] Yet Roy does highlight the importance of certain things, small things—the world of face-to-face interactions. Her characters live in a postcolonial backwater. Traditional oppressions of caste and patriarchy, modern oppressions of racism and colonial legacies, the false promise of Marxism and nationalism, and the ubiquity of international capital and its culture industry are all present in their lives. But their happiness and tragedy are determined not by big structures and processes, which operate as context, but by interactions with each other, by the characters' attempts, not always successful, to create small zones of independence and dignity.

The politics of small things is about constituting such zones. It's the independence that matters, not the size. This suggests another way to consider 9/11 and its challenges. It suggests another way of considering the new sacralized temptation, the official story, and the alternative globalization narrative. In the life of ongoing social institutions and in the forging of social movements, zones of political freedom and creativity are constituted in social interactions, and we must pay attention.

5

2004: Small Things + the Internet = Alternatives

The hero of Arundhati Roy's *God of Small Things*, and his lover, construct space around themselves to establish their individual dignity and shared happiness. Through bearing, demeanor, and breaks with deference they create their own autonomous world, free from the caste order that traditionally would define them. Roy tells a tragic story, but in the space between the lovers she reveals the potential for freedom that is embedded in the small interactions of daily life. This suggests to me that we look to Roy the novelist more than Roy the activist for an understanding of the alternatives to terrorism and antiterrorism. This is the space that Goffman and Arendt, taken together, illuminate. We thus turn to new forms of the politics of small things, to virtual political activism. This requires an understanding that the politics of small things appears in specific political, historical, and media contexts.

In the political realm, it is in that space between people, like the space between Roy's lovers, that the most creative and ultimately consequential alternative to modern tyranny was constructed in the Soviet bloc, especially, as we have observed, in Poland. People acted as if they lived in a free society and a free society resulted. A new political definition of the situation was established. We saw in chapter 2 how that space as a consequential political sphere was created and in chapter 3 how its full development in

Poland, partial development in Czechoslovakia, and almost complete absence in Romania affected the nature of those countries' postcommunist experience.

The politics of small things played a key role in the fall of communism. For the terrorists, the mujahideen, the activities of the Islamic warriors in Afghanistan explain the fall. For the antiterrorist, the key role was played by the anticommunist state, as led by American presidents from Truman to Reagan and Bush senior. But viewed from inside the Soviet bloc, the politics of small things goes a long way toward explaining the fall, especially its democratic character. Now we explore how, in the shadows of the World Trade Center, small things, off the central stage, point to an understanding of alternatives to the dominant presentation of the global conflict between Islamic terrorism and American-defined antiterrorism. I believe that the politics of small things suggest alternative ways to do politics in the aftermath of the attacks of September 11, 2001, no less consequential than such politics in the old Soviet bloc. But to appreciate this, we must understand that we live not only in a new geopolitical order. There is also a new media regime.

The logic of antiterrorism led Bush and Blair into the war in Iraq, a move that was much more controversial on the global stage than the war in Afghanistan, due to its murkier connection with the narrative of antiterrorism. In the opinion of much of the world, the militarization of the war metaphor has undermined the legitimacy of the official narrative of the war on terror. Whereas in the immediate aftermath of the September 11 attacks, there was broad sympathy for the American position there later came to be much antipathy. Supportive critics of the initial policy on the right, such as Kristol, have prevailed. Those on the left, such as Walzer, have been torn between the ideologies of the terrorists and the antiterrorists and, given the configurations of power, have often deemed the antiterrorists to be more dangerous. The willingness of the Bush administration to pursue a new policy of preemptive war, to forego international institutions and pursue a largely unilateral foreign policy, has led to a resurgence of popular anti-Americanism worldwide.

There is much in the criticism of the United States that is unsettling. Many elements in opposition statements are paranoid and profoundly antiliberal and antidemocratic in their implications. Yet the way the antiwar movement has developed, more than the specific positions of specific antiwar activists, suggests a real alternative to the networks of terror and the state response to them. If bin Ladenism is a postmodern variation on the theme of totalitarianism, as I attempted to demonstrate in the last chapter, then the antiwar movement and innovations in political campaigning, most closely associated with the presidential candidacy of Howard Dean, should be understood as revealing postmodern democratic alternatives, postmodern variations on the theme of the politics of small things. Social networks and actions mediated through two Web sites, MoveOn.org and Meetup.com, are clearly discernable virtual locations of a new form of the politics of small things.

The Antiwar Movement and MoveOn

The antiwar movement was created through the Internet. The global reach of the movement and its coordination formed rapidly and intensively. There were major demonstrations throughout the world on February 15, 2003. In New York City, at the epicenter of the 9/11 terrorist attacks, four hundred thousand people marched, and nearly ten million people joined them in demonstrations that spanned the globe. The demonstrations revealed another side of globalization, the capacity to challenge the global superpower democratically. These demonstrations suggest an alternative to terrorism and ideological antiterrorism. A small number of people, using the Internet, helped to coordinate a global citizens response to the impending war. This was a network for the politics of small things, a postmodern alternative to both the empire of globalization and the totalitarian movement of terror. The United for Peace and Justice Web site and MoveOn.org were important virtual spaces for this collective action.

On March 16, a month after the first global demonstration, another protest revealed how the Web could be used in a particularly creative fashion. At dusk, a wave of candlelight vigils moved westward around the earth. One million people, in more than six thousand ceremonies in one hundred thirty different countries, took part. This action was organized by Moveon.org, in six days with five staff people. One participant, Andrew Boyd, describes his involvement:

> The day before that Sunday in March, I went to the MoveOn website, entered my ZIP code and learned that three vigils had been scheduled in my neighborhood of Park Slope, Brooklyn, including one outside the apartment of prowar Senator Chuck Schumer. The website told me how many of my neighbors had signed up for each. It was already well into the hundreds, and I made it one more.
> That Sunday evening, I joined 1,500 of my neighbors. Someone handed me a candle and lit it for me; at some point a rabbi and a pastor spoke to the crowd. But otherwise, there was no ob-

vious leadership, and it didn't seem to matter. There had been no meetings, no leaflets, no clipboards, no phone calls—we were all there, essentially, because of an e-mail we trusted.[1]

This was one of MoveOn's many antiwar initiatives. It has also raised millions of dollars online to finance antiwar ads on television and in print. It presented a petition with one million signatures critical of the war to the UN Security Council. The group had been founded as a response to the impeachment campaign against President Bill Clinton and ever since it has been involved in electoral and Congressional politics and now the antiwar movement. It is a new form of political mobilization, a globalized alternative to both the networks of terrorists and the hegemonic response to that network. As its campaign director, Eli Pariser, has noted, "You could say that MoveOn has a postmodern organizing model. . . . It's opt-in, it's decentralized, you do it from your home."[2]

Meetup and a New Form of Electoral Politics

The meeting tool used by MoveOn, which made it possible for Andrew Boyd and his neighbors to protest the war together locally as part of a global demonstration, has been commercially developed by Meetup.com. The software also was key in developing support of the candidacy of Howard Dean for the Democratic presidential nomination. The antiwar demonstrations were spectacular, representing a new capacity to organize a global public in a coordinated fashion. This organizational capacity may be more significant than the fact that the goals of the movement were not met. The war proceeded without being directly effected by the global protests. But in the case of Democratic politics, this power may have been of greater consequence.

Based on all conventional understandings of American politics, Howard Dean had the makings of an also-ran in the presidential campaign of 2004. He was from a small state in New England. He had no national experience. His strong antiwar stance, his distance from Democratic Party power brokers, and his lack of support from major party donors made it seem even to him that his would be a minimally funded exercise. His harsh criticisms of the incumbent president in a time of war, coupled with sometimes even harsher criticisms of his colleagues in the leadership of the Democratic Party, suggested, according to conventional wisdom, that he was too angry to be a significant force in the primaries. Yet in a relatively short time he became the frontrunner. It became broadly understood that he was the first serious candidate to harness the power of the Internet in presidential electoral politics. If Roosevelt was the first radio president and Kennedy the first television president, for a while it seemed that Dean might become the first Internet president. Even though this did not come to pass, the new type of political power that put Dean on the map is a significant political innovation from the point of view of this inquiry, an electronic form of the politics of small things. With Dean, the medium was the political message. Although he did not win the nomination, the fact that Dean became a significant actor is an important indication of the power of the form of his campaign.

There was a clear, if not completely formalized, link between MoveOn, the Dean campaign, and Meetup. In the summer of 2003 MoveOn held a primary of sorts on its Web site. Three hundred seventeen thousand votes were cast. Dean won 44 percent of the vote, with about twice as many votes as Dennis Kucinich, the runner-up. A centrist governor from a small state outstripped a well-known left-wing member of Congress on a leftist Web site. According to its rules, which required a 50 percent vote, MoveOn did not endorse any candidate. But links were forged between the site and Dean's candidacy nonetheless.

This was first accomplished, not by the organizers of MoveOn or by Dean campaign staff, but by Internet activists. Bloggers, people posting Web logs on the Net, who were associated with the Dean campaign were interlinked with bloggers friendly to MoveOn. Through this connection, Dean's supporters could easily vote in the MoveOn poll. It was made simple. They were encouraged to do so, and they prevailed. This facilitation was not a part of a campaign strategy but rather an outgrowth of personal interactions, in this case virtual interactions, among ordinary people.

It was a creation of the politics of small things. People met each other on the Web. They posted their messages and responded to each other, got to know each other and then coordinated their actions. They redefined the situation, and the situation changed according to their definition. Dean admits, "We fell into this by accident. . . . I wish I could tell you we were smart enough to figure this out. But the community taught us. They seized the initiative through Meetup. They built our organization for us before we had an organization."[3]

Here Dean is referring to the next and crucial part of the process, the connection between virtual and embodied interactions. MoveOn developed its social-movement muscle when it developed the capacity to turn Internet discussions into concerted action. This first involved getting people to sign petitions against the impeachment proceedings and co-ordinating pressure on Congressmen and Congressional candidates on specific issues. As the war in Iraq became an imminent reality, this power moved to organize political demonstrations, linking local interactions with national and international interactions, virtual interactions that led to embodied interactions worldwide. The Dean campaign was organized around this connection between the virtual and the embodied. Meet-ups were at the center of the campaign.

A Closer Look at the New Politics

One gathering organized through Meetup was scheduled for 7:00 p.m. on the first Wednesday of January 2004 in a small city outside of New York. This was one of four meetings in the county, one of sixteen hundred held nationwide and internationally. Fifteen people met at the local headquarters of the Service Employees International Union (a union that had endorsed Dean). Most greeted each other as old friends. They had been gathering in these meetings since the previous summer. There were a few newcomers, who were asked whether they were exploring Dean's candidacy or ready to do work for Dean. Mildly supportive, they responded vaguely. It was explained that the question was asked because the purpose of the meeting was to write personal letters to prospective participants in the Iowa and New Mexico caucuses, encouraging them to take part and to support Dean. They agreed to write letters.

Everyone gathered around a long table. Some bumper stickers, placards, leaflets, and other campaign materials were distributed. People talked among themselves as two leaders organized the formal activities. There were the requisite disparaging remarks about the conventional media. One man made an announcement about a talk being given in the area by Paul Krugman, who to his mind was the only liberal left on the *New York Times* editorial page.

Discussion then turned to foreign policy. One participant challenged another to explain what distinguished the approach of the Democrats from that of the Republicans. There seemed to be general agreement that a commitment to multilateralism was now a key distinction.

One person expressed concern that Dean was not coming across as a person. Voters want to know what sort of person they are being asked to support. To her mind he was still too much of an unknown. The discussion took place at the time when Dean's prospects were faltering. On the eve of the Iowa caucuses, Dean was under relentless attack by the other candidates and these activists shared their concerns.

These people were supporters of Dean, to varying degrees and in different ways. But they shared one common opinion: they were committed to beating George Bush. They had an extremely negative evaluation of the state of affairs in the United States. They were open to other candidates and discussed with each other the desirability of other contenders, considering who was most likely to beat Bush, the first imperative.

But if they were open to other candidates, they were deeply committed to the process in which they were engaged. A call came in from Dean headquarters in Burlington, Vermont. Buses were being organized to go to New Hampshire to canvass there in the coming weeks. All expenses would be paid. If people could get themselves to Iowa, again their expenses would be paid and places to stay would be arranged. The person on the other end of the line asked if there were any questions. There were a few about housing arrangements, details of transportation possibilities, meals.

The members of the group chatted with each other as they wrote their letters. Each person composed handwritten notes to one voter in Iowa and one in New Mexico. The task was to encourage people in these two states to take part in their caucuses. There were guidelines, but the people composed their own notes. Tens of thousands of these letters were being written on this one night across the country. Dean has received a lot of attention concerning his fund-raising prowess. But that is only the most apparent manifestation of a new way of doing politics.

The letter writers met through Meetup.com and the Internet but came to know each other through face-to-face interactions. They were also connected to a traditional political campaign via telephone and campaign directives, such as the guidelines for letter writing. But they wrote the notes in their own hand, in their own words. The latest innovations of the information age brought people together in the most basic form of social life. They were linked through modern technology and social organization, through the telephone and the political party organization, and in the end through a form of communication that predates the industrial age: the postal system and the handwritten letter. Each media element was meaningful, including the informal conversation that continued as participants wrote their letters.

The chat was about the politics of the day. People shared with each other their excitement about their involvement and their concern about the course of the campaign. The activists around the table introduced themselves. Among them were a local politician, old radical veterans, a clerical worker and her friend, a college student, an artist, and two professors (including me). Most had never before been involved in electoral politics. They were more excited about the Dean campaign than about the candidate. They were taking part in political life at a time of deep concern, and they were clearly energized by the experience. They were doing something relatively mundane, but the fact that they had recruited themselves, and that they knew that others of like mind throughout the nation had also done so and that this was having an effect, was very exciting to them. They understood that something new was occurring and that they were part of it.

This sense of political creativity and empowerment was common in the face-to-face Meetup gatherings but also something that was shared virtually over a more extended domain. A whole world of involvement was available to the Dean activist: e-mail bulletins and exchanges, fund-raising updates and requests, invitations to future meet-ups and campaign parties. Activists met together to watch primary results, the Super Bowl, and the State of the Union address, and they raised funds and planned strategy for future activities while they enjoyed each other's company. They formed affective ties to each other and to the campaign. Activists read and posted on message boards comments concerning strategy and substantive issues, reviews of the candidates' performances and positions, criticisms of the mass media. These were organized by the campaign and through dozens, perhaps hundreds, of other sources, many of which were interlinked with the official campaign Web site. There was a community of intimate interaction that crossed media formats and physical space. Instrumental activity and social bonds together formed a new sort of political power.

New Politics, Old Media

Beyond fund-raising and the actual campaign, this new political power effectively influenced how the established broadcast and print media function. A new interactive dimension was added to the political world. Groups linked with but not officially part of the campaign organized themselves in various ways: as the Dean Rapid Response Network, which monitored and responded to media reports on the candidate, and as groups on Yahoo.com that monitored national and state media and sent summaries and links to articles and broadcasts about the candidate to network members via e-mail. Some messages were simply informational. Others included negative or positive responses. Members responded, sending e-mails and letters to media organizations, whose addresses were provided, and the media's responses were shared on the network's boards. This monitoring did make sloppy and aggressively negative reporting more difficult. For better and worse, it probably provided some incentive to avoid negative bias and to present more favorable coverage. More assuredly, it established an interactive community among those who posted and who read the posts. They became a virtual public that turned the one-way broadcaster-audience relationship into an exchange. Through their concerted action, thousands of media reports were subjected to this type of transformation.

In early January, Dean's campaign was beginning to falter. He was the clear frontrunner, and other candidates were attacking. He was being subjected to very critical media scrutiny, and his rhetorical style was negatively evaluated as being unpresidential. One statement he made seemed particularly wild and damaging. In an interview on National Public Radio, Dean speculated about President Bush's foreknowledge of the 9/11 attacks. Paula Zahn of CNN reported: "Let me just repeat exactly what came off the transcript of the NPR radio show. And this is Governor Dean's remark—quote—'The most interesting theory that I have heard so far,' he responded—quote—'is that he was warned ahead of time by the Saudis.'"[4] Where Zahn broke the quote with "he responded," she cut out a crucial part of what Dean had said: "which is nothing more than a theory, I can't think—it can't be proved." Thus Dean's complete sentence during the NPR interview was: "The most interesting theory that I have heard so far, which is nothing more than a theory, I can't think—it can't be proved, is that he was warned ahead of time by the Saudis." Dean was not asserting that Bush knew of the attacks before hand. He was thinking out loud in an unguarded fashion about how critical people were thinking about the attacks. It may not have been particularly wise for a candidate to make such a statement to the national media. But the selective dropping of the qualifying portion of the statement transformed its meaning. That Dean was clearly distancing himself from the theory was suggested by the clause Zahn omitted. This is an example of selective distortion. The edited sentence fit into the story line that depicted Dean as not presidential and his campaign as losing its focus. Liz Herbert, a particularly active member of the Dean rapid response group, posted this explanation of the CNN report. Network volunteers then responded to this and other messages about media reporting, which they received on a daily basis. In state and national groups they become a community, capable of significant media intervention. The major media outlets were affected by these interventions, as were political actors in the field.

The claim of Fox News that it is fair and balanced is easy for liberals to reject. Its talk shows are decidedly right-wing. Its reporting is, from the liberals' point of view, biased: clearly prowar, pro-Bush, pro-Republican, as is its owner and its chief executive. The rapid response group went beyond such categorical judgment. They monitored the network's programs systematically, catching reporters and commentators in clear inaccuracies and distortions.

On September 12, 2003, Fox News reported:

> Dean has been under fire for suggesting the United States should
> not take sides in the Middle East conflict and Israel should get out
> of disputed territories of the West Bank.

In a news alert that day a network activist observed, "This subtle spin
makes it sound as if he's anti-Israel." Fox went on to observe that "while
he has insisted that he backs U.S. policy supporting Israel, statements
made on Wednesday about Hamas raise new questions." The network activist countered, "What questions? They never say. They just want to create intangible doubt." And when Fox concluded that "Dean condemned
terrorism but his description of Hamas—designated by the United States
as a terrorist group—as 'soldiers in a war' conflicts with U.S. policy," the
activist noted that the "unspoken lie here is the suggestion that Dean supports Hamas" and concluded: "They also fail to mention the co-opting
of the word 'war' by conservatives for political purposes."

The Dean network's alert concluded with a call for Dean supporters
to respond:

> Please write to the editor and point out the writer's political bias.
> Mention that you are not fooled by his covert attempts to create
> doubt about Dean's positions, and that he insults the intelligence
> of the readers by attempting to do so. Be cordial and formal, but
> let your position be known. Read up on the facts carefully before
> responding.

It then gave an e-mail address for Fox News and links to a statement on
Middle East policy on the Dean campaign Web site and a definition of *sol-
dier* ("militant follower of an organization") from an online dictionary.

There is much that is noteworthy in this, to begin with its intelligence
and the connection of intelligence with a clear path for social action. This
is not simply a partisan moaning that Fox News is not fair to his candidate. Rather, there is a close reading of the report, a guide to understanding precisely how it distorts, and a careful statement of how the
members of the network should respond, with links provided for more
information. It is then up to the members to act, and they do.

One can be cynical about the point of this when it comes to Fox. This
is not an outlet that was likely to be favorable to Dean. Its "fair and balanced" slogan, from the point of view of the Dean candidacy and Democrats more generally, is belied by its clearly coming from the right side

of the political spectrum. But the effect can be more apparent in the case of news outlets that are less tendentious, such as the one that claims to publish "All the News That is Fit to Print," the *New York Times.*

The *Times*'s ombudsman and public editor, Daniel Okrent, whose job is to be the public critic of the *Times* within the *Times,* wrote about the mass of letters the paper received about its political reporting on Dean.[5] He noted: "Nearly every time there's a story about Dean in the paper, my in-box fills with complaints from his fans. (Every time there isn't a story providing a precis of a new policy statement from the Dean camp, it is almost the same.)" He then quoted from a number of the letters and offered his assessment. He noted the vehemence of some of the letters but then reviewed the complaints and the reporting, observing that "the paper has made mistakes," and concluded, "That's what I found in seven weeks of intense coverage: one sentence; one picture; two headlines; and an overplayed story." In his final judgment, the supporters of Dean had something to criticize, but they needed to realize that the scrutiny directed at Dean and the volume of reports on him were a consequence of his ascendancy in the electoral field. He was the subject of many more reports than the other candidates, something they complained about. Okrent concluded that there had been minor mistakes but nothing systematically wrong with the reports.

The interaction with the media was ongoing. That same day someone on the response network noted the article approvingly: "This is great that the NY Times is taking an honest look at their coverage of Dean. Please write to thank them for that. This is also a great opportunity to make any points about the coverage you feel they aren't addressing, explain from your personal perspective where the frustration comes from."[6] This is a small sample of literally thousands of exchanges that appear on the Dean Web log and associated blogs. Some of them, such as the ones I just highlighted, were very intelligent, some not.

The Dean campaign began to collapse in Iowa. He was expected to win. Until two weeks before the caucuses, the expectation was that it would be a battle between him and Richard Gephardt, the industrial union strength of Gephardt versus the Internet strength of Dean. Getting supporters to the caucuses, the conventional wisdom suggested, is the key to victory in Iowa. The old-fashioned capacity of the unions to get out the vote for a candidate from Missouri, a neighboring state, was understood to be formidable, and that would be pitted against the new forces of virtual organization, bringing thousands of young volunteers from elsewhere to knock on doors and help Dean supporters get to the caucus meetings. In the end, Dean came in third, with only 18 percent of the vote, and Gephardt fourth, with 11 percent, leading him to withdraw from the race. Dean and his supporters were profoundly disappointed.

The defeat threw the campaign off. When the results came in, Dean met his supporters in Iowa. He gave a speech that was widely viewed as being situationally inappropriate. He shouted, barked, and bellowed when quiet reflection and respectful concession seemed to be the order of the moment. He declared: "We're going to South Carolina and Oklahoma and Arizona and North Dakota and New Mexico. We're going to California and Texas and New York!" After listing more states, finishing with Washington D.C., the *New York Times* reported, he "punctuated the speech with a throaty howl."[7] Both his supporters and Democratic Party analysts reacted with consternation. Dean's performance became the object of relentless ridicule, dubbed by NPR's Robert Siegel the "I had a scream speech."[8]

The response on pro-Dean Web sites varied. Some people posted critical comments about the candidate's speech and the campaign, even reservations about continuing to support him given the oddity of his speech and his belligerent way of presenting it. Others posted comments that revealed the loyalty of Dean's supporters. The following excerpts were posted on January 21. The first comes from the Dean Rapid Response Network, the rest from the Dean for America Web site:

> As for Dean's supposed over the top battle-cry, if you're embarrassed by it then you've played right into the Repug/Media Whore hands. Every candidate has done things that have been a bit embarrassing. Remember the big fuss about Kerry asking for Swiss cheese on his Philly steak sandwich? How many times did you see that on the news ad nauseam . . . didn't seem to effect his Iowa numbers, did it? The same thing goes with Dean's battle-cry. Was it a bit over the top? Sure, but as usual the only ones making a big deal out of it, and who even care are the loud-mouthed pundits. (Mike Jones, "Re: What happened?")

> *

> Dean's Iowa night speech, in my opinion, was impassioned and was meant for his supporters. He probably, in the moment, forgot that he was also expected to address the nation. I think that's forgivable. He's rallying his troops and he did it with real passion. REAL passion. He feels it, and that's important. So what if he can't yell "Yeah" without sounding nutty. That was the end of a long motivating speech. He lost his voice in hoarseness. Did you see his posture? Did you hear (or even read transcripts) of the whole

event? He's out in the open talking to his people, not hiding stiffly behind a podium spouting expletives (which is how some are painting it).

As E. M. Forster once put it, "One person with passion is better than forty people merely interested." (benchwarmer, "Governor Dean's Speech in Iowa")

*

Wow, I just don't get it. I watched the post-Iowa speech with my girlfriend last night and we found it to be very moving. In fact, it was almost tear jerking to see the sincerity pour out of Dean to his supporters. Seeing that speech inspired me to do even more for the campaign frankly. When we saw the press run with this "he was absolutely out of control" rhetoric, I just didn't understand it. Seriously, Dean did nothing wrong. However, I am even more frustrated with some of these so-called Dean supporters for giving this already pathetic, tabloid spun "gotcha" story even more legs by posting impressionable distortions like some Dean supporters did here.

Most international news sources described the American coverage of Dean's post-Iowa speech story as being an "obvious low blow spin job" In short, the fickle could stand to read more international news.

Ya know Clinton only got 3% of Iowa. What kind of world do we live in where passion and sincerity are called "crazy" and the overly scripted, sociopathic traits are "normal"?

When I started supporting Dean last summer, I knew it was gonna be a hard battle, and I knew that the major American media was gonna try to distort who Howard really is. This is a time to get louder, prouder, stronger, and smarter!

Dean can count on me till the end! Let's triple Meetup attendance! Put up flyers in your cities, towns of where and when your Meetup is!!! LET'S TAKE OUR COUNTRY BACK FROM SPECIAL INTERESTS, BUSH INC & DLC INSIDERS! We can do it, we have more than enough resources to win. We've already made the impossible possible on many levels, don't forget that! (Astronautagogo, "Open Letter to All Fickle Critics")

*

Yah, well, I have a different take. I thought it was very embarrassing and very poor judgement, but forgivable ONLY because it was to his supporters. My wife saw it at the same time, and she was absolutely, absolutely mortified. The yell at the end was petrifying. It was the first time she had seen him on TV, and it has poisoned her for good. Yah, he'll shake it off I guess, but that was one heck of a bad way to introduce himself to voters. (Mark Olson, "Open Letter to All Fickle Critics")

The debate raged. While not consequential in and of itself, it was the ongoing discussion of an engaged citizenry. People spoke with passion to each other. They agreed, disagreed, and prepared themselves for common action. Hundreds of posts were made on dozens of threads as people attached themselves to this social movement.

And this was reported in the media. The *New York Times* report on the speech concluded with a message posted on the official Web site of the Dean campaign: "A message from someone with the email title AltDem wrote, 'I hate to say it, but Gov looked downright scary tonight.'"[9] This of course was discussed further on the site, and so forth.

The Politics of Small Things in the New Media Constellation

The notion that Dean was the Internet candidate misses an important point. It suggests that the Internet was his instrument, which he used with mixed results. Roosevelt used radio. Kennedy used television. And in 2004 Dean used the Internet. This overlooks the rich interconnections between media forms. More precisely, it misses the way that social interactions facilitated by different media create political power. The power that was constituted by the Dean campaign was an outgrowth of a layered, differentiated, but common dimension of power, political power as the capacity for people to meet, speak, and act in the presence of others, developing a capacity for concerted action. Having considered the historical narrative of the development of such power, we now view it from our alternative theoretical perspective, from the perspective of Hannah Arendt and Erving Goffman.

A key to the importance of the politics of small things, as we have seen, is the power of definition. People, when they meet and talk with each other, have to define the terms of their discussion and can, in the process, change the world. The international demonstrations organized by MoveOn, along with its other political activities, presented an alternative definition of the situation after the attacks of 9/11. The terrorists defined the situation as one of jihad. The antiterrorists spoke about the axis of evil. The movement facilitated by MoveOn, embodied in what were probably the largest antiwar demonstrations in world history, defined the situation in a very different way. The movement was truly globalized.

The participants came to the demonstrations committed to different things, with different and often competing understandings of the world situation. To be sure, there were people who understood the situation in terms of an antiglobalization theme. Roy and Chomsky were most certainly popular authors among those who demonstrated. Yet the form of the demonstrations was more important in understanding their meaning than the specific political commitments of the participants.

There was no single manifesto that united all the demonstrators. The common commitment was minimal. A worldwide "no" to the war on terrorism, as defined by George W. Bush and his allies and as extended to the war in Iraq, was articulated. In France this position was continuous with the position of the national government, as was also the case in Brazil, South Africa, Mexico, Germany and many other places. In the United States, the demonstrations were directed against officialdom, as they were in Italy, Australia, Spain, Poland, and the other countries in the "coalition of the willing." Some held the conviction that this was the latest instance of American imperialism, the view of Chomsky and his supporters. They saw a definite continuity with the foreign adventures of the cold war era, and even of the Clinton administration. For others what was striking was the break with the policy of supporting human rights of recent years. Some protested in support of an Arab nation and its sovereignty, a Muslim nation beset by the demonic West. Others thought merely that this war of liberation was miscalculated, fought without sufficient legitimation by the international community, the people of the region, and the Western democracies. This last group opposed the war not because it was a manifestation of globalization but because it was not sufficiently globalized.

The diversity of people's motivations for participating in the protest did place a limitation on common action. The site of Not in Our Name, a central antiwar group, maintains a list of organizations supporting antiwar activities, with links to their Web sites. Two clicks beyond this page, one starts to discern the range of positions. There is Electronic Intifada, a Web site that provides a Palestinian perspective on the Middle East conflict, next to which is Revolutionary Worker on Line, the site of a Maoist party with an early-twentieth-century appeal. Another site provides commentary by Michael Moore, an article by Arundhati Roy on the new American century excerpted from the *Nation*, and pieces by *Times* columnist Paul Krugman, Vermont representative Bernie Sanders, and dozens of others. Every conceivable position critical of the war can be found very rapidly, and all were represented in the worldwide demonstrations. Individual interactions facilitated by the Web peopled and coordinated the demonstrations, but given the differences between the many groups' positions, the possibility for common action was limited. They could do only one thing together. They could say no to the war, and no more. Anything beyond that, and the coalition would splinter.

There is an analogy to be made to the demonstrations in Romania in 1989. There, the history of repression made it so that the atomized members of a totalitarian order could say little to the powers other than "no." In the case of the globalized antiwar demonstrators, the thinness of their virtual connections yielded a similar result. Their connections were not embodied. They could disappear as rapidly as they appeared. They covered broad sectors of the population linked by the vectors of global communications but with otherwise limited interconnections.[10] Participants in the demonstrations did not share substantive positions beyond opposition to the war. In sum, the interactions that facilitate the development of political power were severely limited in the antiwar movement in a way that was similar to the limitations in Bucharest in 1989.

Dean's political campaign addressed many of these issues and provided a form for the politics of small things to develop more fully. When compared to other global communications media—print, film, radio, and television—the interconnectivity of the Web is very impressive. This new global communication system is distinguished from the older forms by the greater importance of small interactions. But the Dean campaign went further in showing how the Web can lead to a fully developed political agency.

Fund-raising capacity, while not insignificant, was only the most apparent manifestation. Other political candidates have also used the Internet to tap the capacity of small contributors to fuel a candidacy. John McCain did so in the elections of 2000. But Dean revealed what might be called the mirror image of the principle of taxation. Given the shape of income distribution, it is not the rich but those in the middle who provide the solid base for government revenues. Dean managed to raise funds for campaigning that reproduced that pattern. Using the broad support of many small contributors, he freed his candidacy from dependence upon very wealthy contributors. Given that campaign contributions have undermined American democracy, this change in fund-raising has potentially transformative implications for democracy in America. With financial support goes political influence.

But even more significant is that the Dean campaign was organized around small social interactions. When Dean explained that he was a product of his supporters' activities, rather than their being a product of his campaign strategy and organization, he was expressing a truth that went beyond the usual gestures of democratic leadership. It was discrete small virtual interactions among people on the MoveOn site and independent bloggers supporting Dean that turned him into the major antiwar candidate. Much of the campaign and people's attachment to the campaign proceeded from the active involvement of supporters with the Dean Web site.

This raised some concerns: People were just preaching and speaking to the converted. Competing positions were not being confronted. Bruce Bimber, a scholar of online campaigning, asserts, "Democracy has been defined as a process of discussion. . . . The internet's tendency to fragment people into like-minded groups is something those of us who study these things are worried about."[11] There is a concern by activists and observers alike that the Internet is balkanizing political discourse and that, as a consequence, public discourse and democratic capacity are being undermined.

But this misses a crucial point. Discussions on the Dean Web sites and other partisan Web sites were not the general public sphere, conceptualized by Jurgen Habermas, where all citizens discuss the problems of the day and come to understand each other, seeking a common course of action.[12] Rather they constituted a place for the politics of small things, where people met each other, came to know and trust each other, and developed a capacity, through a shared definition of the situation, to engage in a common course of action. It is such "speaking to the converted" that makes it possible to go beyond the "no" of the antiwar movement, that makes it possible in networks of virtual interaction to raise money, monitor the mass media, and plan in a decentralized fashion a political campaign. The interaction was virtual but often quite familiar, even in a sense intimate.

Maureen Dowd wrote a tart op-ed piece in the *New York Times* on Howard Dean. It had all the elements of her writing, ironic, even cynical commentary based on the observation of style. She expressed regret that "Howard Dean's bark was missing its bite. His socks were missing their warp. Not to mention their woof."[13] She observed that Dean had tried to recalibrate his presentation, to soften the hard edges, after the "I had a scream" speech. She mocked his television appearances on CBS's *Late Show with David Letterman* and on ABC's *Primetime Live,* where he and his wife were interviewed by Diane Sawyer. Dowd noted the stylistic deficiencies of Dean and his wife, their disdain for television viewing, and other oddities. It was a light piece, with an edge. Dean and his wife are northeastern liberals, distanced from popular obsessions with celebrity and style.

The members of the New York rapid response team were critical. Samuel Pratt wrote a letter to the *Times* on the day Dowd's column was published and shared it with the members of the Yahoo Dean network: "Enough with the yelping and hissing and climbing on the ropes even after your opponent is down for the count."[14] The *Times* responded later that day with a polite dismissal, which Pratt also posted: "Unless there's evidence of ethical misbehavior or factual error, individual columnists can say what they want to say and individual readers can like the ones they like and dislike the ones they don't like." This was followed by two posts congratulating Pratt for a job well done.

This sort of exchange is a sample of the interactive building block of Dean's power—the intervention in the public world, followed by a confirmation of social support from those inside the movement. It is the virtual equivalent of the patterns of deference and demeanor that established the tenor of the underground poetry reading in Warsaw in the late 1970s. These patterns served to define that event as a normal one, as an independent cultural setting such as might exist in a free society. When the setting persisted and escaped repression such a free society came to be established. On the threads and blogs concerned with the Dean candidacy the same sort of social activity was rendered virtually. There was a clear professionalism in the way the official campaign blog was presented. And those who met through blogs, chat groups, and self-organized groups using Yahoo and Meetup developed friendships, acted in each other's presence, built a shared view of the world, and defined and judged events together. Then, based on these shared definitions and judgments, they acted. In such a way a social movement mediated through virtual communication was established, a social movement that was capable of refined judgments and precise political interventions that went well beyond the power of saying no.

Internet Bubble?

Because the Dean campaign did not prevail, there is a temptation to dismiss the political efficacy of virtually constituted political power, the politics of small things online. Three days after his defeat in New Hampshire, the *New York Times* asserted on its editorial page: "Howard Dean's implosion calls to mind the fate of too many high-flying dot-com companies in the wake of the 2000–2001 crash. Dr. Dean relished being anointed as the Internet presidential candidate last year, when he was riding high, but now the title is proving disconcertingly prophetic."[15]

There may have been problems with the Dean campaign. Perhaps some of them had to do with an overestimation of what the new medium could accomplish in isolation from more traditional media, but the fact remains that Dean managed to launch a credible campaign and that the problems that ended that campaign included very traditional ones: Funds were mismanaged.[16] The strategy of spending heavily on a national level early, extensively, and intensively in hopes of a quick knockout did not work. Internet money flowed in freely, but it flowed out as quickly to pay for advertising and campaign salaries. The candidate's infamous scream speech weakened him just at the wrong time, but that was just one instance of a series of miscues in television presentations. The candidate did not work on making himself appear likable. He presented positions but not personality. Given the continued centrality of television, this was a key mistake.[17] Too many people did not like Al Gore in 2000, could not bear the prospect of having him in their living rooms, kitchens, and bedrooms on a daily basis. He was stiff, aggressive, condescending. While he did win the popular vote and some think that he should have won the electoral college,[18] he certainly did not win as decisively as would be expected given the state of the economy, the geopolitical situation at the time, and the popularity of the president under whom he had served as vice president. Not enough people liked him enough to vote for him. With this in mind, there was an imperative for the Democratic candidate to have good rapport with the voters, but Dean did not work on this.

The power of the politics of small things working through virtual interactions does not replace other ways of generating power in the contemporary media landscape. The power of television cannot be denied. But that does not mean that this new form of the politics of small things is insignificant. First, we should remember that it helped transform the governor of a small state with little prospect of competing into a real player in the conventional political contest. Much more was involved, though, as is quite evident when we put this instance of the politics of small things into a broader political context.

When people demonstrated worldwide against the war in Iraq, only the most marginal participants could imagine it would have the effect of taking state power. The reasonable end was straightforward: to voice worldwide disapproval of the war and to turn public opinion and political leaders against it. The demonstrations were highly successful. They probably go a long way toward explaining the steadfast resistance of many United Nations members to the position of the global superpower, and they serve as the globalized cultural context for the postwar struggles in Iraq. But the protests were a blunt instrument, the effects of which cannot be demonstrated. As with speculation about the significance of the anti–Vietnam war movement, judgments about their effects very much depend upon the position of the judge.

But when the politics of small things went beyond the power of saying no, when it became the grounds for Dean's presidential candidacy, the consequences of the actions became much clearer. One of Dean's most appealing initial assertions was his statement that he is from "the Democratic wing of the Democratic Party." He was expressing the dismay of Democrats that their party had lost its way. It had not effectively challenged the neoliberal, antistatist domestic agenda of the right wing of the Republican Party for a very long time, in some senses since the ascendancy of Ronald Reagan, and it was not challenging the militarized antiterrorist campaign of George W. Bush. Dean's candidacy, as an outgrowth of the antiwar movement, changed this. He forthrightly opposed Bush's policies in Iraq and in the war on terrorism, and as a result the developing antiwar virtual polity adopted him. Between his message and their formation of a social movement using the politics of small things, he became a political force to be reckoned with. On domestic issues, he forthrightly criticized tax cuts proposed by Bush and ratified by the Congress that were overwhelmingly favorable to the wealthy and disadvantageous to the poor.[19] Those cuts, combined with increased military expenditures on the wars in Afghanistan and Iraq and the general war on terrorism, created huge federal deficits that undermined the possibility of addressing pressing problems in education, health care, and increasing impoverishment. The Democrats in Congress were rather timid in addressing these issues in the midterm elections of 2002. Through his candidacy Dean addressed them, and forced all the other candidates for president to address them.

This points to the most striking achievement of the politics of small things in the age of terrorism and antiterrorism: a change in the political discourse. Since the communist collapse, systematic criticism of the truisms of the right had become difficult. As socialism, the systemic alternative to capitalism, came to appear unworkable and as the welfare state revealed its own systemic problems, the neoliberal right came to appear sensible, while the left most often did not.[20] It was not that neoliberalism was the only way to proceed, or the best way, and it was not that history really had come to an end, as the turmoil of recent years has cogently re-

vealed. Rather, it was that alternatives to neoliberalism, and for that
matter fundamentalism, were not being clearly and consequentially articulated.

For a while it appeared as if the Anglo-Americans had teamed up to
present an alternative. Much as Reagan and Margaret Thatcher were the
politicians who made the new right-wing common sense prevail, it seemed
that Clinton and Blair were pointing to a new third way, a way that
adapted to the persuasiveness of the critique of the welfare state and to
the historical collapse of socialism, that utilized the creativity and pro-
ductiveness of a market economy but did not give up on the pursuit of social justice. But Clinton's poor management of the health-care debate and
his policy of political triangulation, situating himself between the Republicans and Congressional Democrats on social issues, coupled with
the scandals surrounding his sexual escapades, derailed this possibility, at
least in the United States. In Latin America, most interestingly in Brazil,
democratic alternatives to neoliberalism and statism have begun to appear, and in Europe such alternatives seem to be forthcoming. But in the
United States, this had not been the case until Dean came on the scene.

Even though Dean's personal quest failed, the great significance of his
candidacy is that he helped redefine the Democratic Party. It is now more
clearly the party concerned with social justice for the poor. This became
the thrust of the candidacy of John Edwards. It is the party that confronts
the militarized approach to the war on terrorism. This was the position
of all the Democratic candidates other than Joseph Lieberman during the
primaries, and it was the central appeal of John Kerry and Wesley Clark,
along with Dean. It is the party that promotes a systematic reform of
medical insurance, a position promoted by all the candidates but especially Dean and Dick Gephardt. And it is the party that fundamentally
questions the way the war in Iraq was declared and the conduct of the
American occupation. Again this was the position of all the candidates
but Lieberman.

The United States has long been without a political alternative to the
positions of the neoliberals and the fundamentalists. Liberal Democrats
have been marginalized, as self-identified centrists move the party away
from basic alternative principles. The alternative now exists because of
the candidacy of Dean, or more precisely because of the way the politics
of small things created space for political freedom and redefinition in the
American political landscape. People met and talked to each other, often
virtually, and developed a capacity for concerted action. They redefined
the situation, and power was constituted. A renewed democratic voice

could be heard. A more serious dialogue about pressing issues of the day became a part of mainstream politics, the politics of the two-party system. This was a significant political development.

Yet the critical voice was not heard clearly enough by the majority of the American electorate. That is another reason why the virtual politics of small things, as constituted by Democratic activists, can be questioned and has been overlooked: it did not prevail in the general elections.

6

2004: The Church, the Right, and the Politics of Small Things

The limits of the new politics of small things were apparent as the presidential election came to a conclusion in November of 2004. John Kerry ran a campaign that clearly distinguished the Democrats from the Republicans, very much informed by the successful aspects of the Dean campaign. He rallied all the Democrats' forces of support, mobilized his core constituency. Using the Internet, he more than matched the Republicans in fund-raising. But he lost. This led to despair and confusion among those who supported him and who were looking for alternatives to the new political order of George W. Bush and company.

Much of the commentary that followed speculated about limitations of Kerry's candidacy. Writers pointed to his personality and politics, to his limited regional appeal, to his running too much as a liberal or, conversely, not enough as a liberal. Immediately after the election, "moral issues" appeared to be decisive. In the National Election Pool exit poll, it was most frequently cited as the one determining factor in electoral choice, by 22 percent of the voters. It was followed by the economy and jobs (20 percent), terrorism (19 percent), Iraq (15 percent), health care (8 percent), taxes (5 percent), and education (4 percent). Even more significant, of those who cited moral issues, 80 percent voted for President Bush. Later, closer analysis

indicated weaknesses in these figures. They were forced by the same ques-
tionable polling techniques that led to early projections of Kerry as the
winner. The category of moral values included many different commitments, not necessarily only the values of religious conservatives. There
was little evidence that a greater proportion of religious people than of
the general public voted.[1]

Yet more people than usual did vote. Intense mobilizations by Democrats and Republicans both contributed to the increased turnout. The
religious right seemed to match and surpass the efforts of the Democrats.
This suggests that the Democrats lost a simple political contest. The Republicans beat them in the race to engage their core constituencies. It also
points to an important theoretical question. Was the politics of small
things just as important in supporting the status quo in the United States,
including its war policies, as in the search for alternatives? The politics of
small things may have reinvigorated a sacralized politics of the right, as
much as or even more than a secularized politics of the left. Social interactions in evangelical churches during the election of 2004 suggest the
importance of micropolitics for the religious right in the United States.
As the politics of small things gave voice to the left, the opposing voice of
the religious right was also clearly articulated, and supported by ordinary
people in their daily lives.

Micropolitics and the Religious Right

The mobilization and fund-raising drives through the Internet of the antiwar movement and the Dean campaign had their mirror images in the
churches and other institutions of the religious right. In fact, the left's
success at broad popular mobilization was a response to popular media
innovations by the right that date back to the Reagan years.[2] As the election approached and as it became clear that it was going to be close, the
question arose: which side would mobilize its supporters more successfully and consequently win the election? Although there is no single factor that explains the outcome, the successful mobilization of religious
voters on the right certainly contributed.

That interactions among people fostered change in political life is of
central importance. While the social interactions inside and among
churches amplified the strength of the dominant instead of presenting an
alternative to them, they still did apparently constitute an independent
political force, one that may have significant impact on the greater society.

The politics of small things can just as readily support the status quo
or prevailing trends as oppose them. In Arendt's depiction of the free pol-

itics of antiquity, this was the case. People came together. They discussed the fate of and defended the polis. Politics was about sustaining the political order of freedom as it was commonly understood. Clearly those of the Christian right think this is exactly what they are doing.

There has been a real parallel between the micropolitics of the left and right on the American scene. On the left, Rock the Vote and similar projects sought to move young voters who were likely to be against Bush. On the right, there was Redeem the Vote, which was supportive of the Christian president. Both of these organizations were officially nonpartisan enterprises, affiliated with other nonpartisan organizations.[3] Yet Rock the Vote was headed by a former Democratic National Committee director and supported by such organizations as the United Service Employees International Union, a very progressive union. Redeem the Vote was staffed by students from Patrick Henry College, an extremely conservative institution, and was endorsed by key figures of the religious right, including Gary Bauer, James Dobson, and Charles Colson. Its partners included the Christian Broadcasting Network, Focus on the Family, and Fox News. Major pop artists with clear political agendas supported Rock the Vote, among them the Dixie Chicks and Public Enemy. Christian rappers and rockers supported Redeem the Vote. Both were clearly directed to get out a partisan portion of the youth vote using the expressive appeal of celebrity.

There were other major nationwide organizations on the right that challenged the popular antiwar movement and the Dean campaign. The right and left organizations were similar in form. The Christian Coalition describes itself as "America's Leading Grassroots Organization Defending Our Godly Heritage."[4] Just as MoveOn and like organizations helped organize the left around such general principles as providing an alternative to the foreign and domestic policies of the right, the Christian Coalition (and like organizations) formulated its positions in opposition to the "godless" tendencies it recognized in American society. It opened its Web site with a call to action:

> Today Christians are playing an active role in the government again by uniting and standing up for people of faith. Hundreds of pro-family political leaders have been elected to local and state and federal office. Pro-family activism is changing policy and influencing decisions from school boards all the way to the US Congress. You can help by joining us.
>
> Add your voice to the millions across America who have said it's time for people of faith to speak up and become involved.

With your help, innocent human lives will no longer go unpro-
tected by our laws, more public schools will meet minimum standards, and fewer of our young people will be snared by drugs, violence and sexual promiscuity.

Your becoming involved means that Christian Coalition of
America can distribute more voter guides and scorecards, train
more activists and sway more critical votes in Congress and the
states. By joining us, you won't just sway one vote—you will impact America forever.

It went on to highlight three ways to make a difference: being a role model
by becoming a "prayer coordinator," praying for the nation daily by starting a Christian Coalition chapter, or becoming involved in an existing
chapter. In the purview of their daily lives, the coalition was maintaining,
individuals can make a difference, easily and effectively.

This suggested activism resembled the virtual activism of the antiwar
movement and the Dean campaign, with an important difference. The
link between the individual and the large-scale movement was centered
on a specific local setting, the church and affiliated organizations. As *Religion in the News* reporter Kimberly Conger observes, "Activists on the
religious right have known each other for years and likely live in the same
town, sit together on mission boards, have children who go to the
same Christian schools and Christian colleges, and support the same chari-
table organizations. These people are friends, and they are connected to
each other in ways that go far beyond politics."[5]

This grounding in local, everyday practices is an important strength
of the Christian right. It presented real tactical advantages during the
elections. The Republicans achieved their mobilization goals through the
work of friends and neighbors, while it was more often through the work
of strangers that the Democrats tried to achieve theirs. When campaign
workers organized through meet-ups approached potential voters, they
generally did not know the people they were meeting. On the religious
right, though, campaign workers and potential voters were likely members of the same church and community organizations.

In light of democratic ideals, this close connection with the community does pose problems. The political mobilization in 2004 was embedded in and directed from an institution that is not democratic in principle
or in practice. Religious leaders were key actors in the movement,[6] and
they claim a superior authority when it comes to God, perhaps within
their congregations and certainly when it comes to nonbelievers or be-

lievers who believe differently. Ministers' relationships with their community as dominant authoritative figures in itself challenges democratic principle. When people came together in churches and engaged in politics large and small, there was a danger that the authority of revelation would replace democratic interaction. Consider the following report:

> Religion and politics sit side by side on a table outside the sanctuary at Akron Baptist Temple—a book on "The Passion of the Christ" next to a stack of election voter guides. From the pulpit, Reverend Dallas Billington had a message for the faithful. "Vote your Bible."[7]

The religious message of the church and the politics of the republic were brought closely together by the pastor. He guided his flock not only religiously, but also politically. This was controversial on constitutional grounds, particularly as it was linked with a national partisan strategy and with government policies. It also introduces a strikingly predemocratic, premodern character into American politics. This was the politics of a deferential society, where a community leader made an informed judgment on matters of public concern and his inferiors complied with his decisions. This was the framework of eighteenth-century American politics, the framework that the founders imagined but that the dynamics of a market and democratic society replaced.[8]

Consider other reports:

> The Reverend Ken Hutcherson's game plan is simple. The former professional football player turned mega church pastor intends to pack a stadium-size crowd of evangelical Christians onto the [Washington, D.C., National] Mall today to decry same-sex marriage and "let everyone know that God is in control" of the 2004 presidential elections.[9]

> *

> My job is to get pastors and Christian people to understand their responsibility to vote and to know the issues that are important as it relates to the divine sovereign.[10]

There is a presumption here that the evangelical minister somehow knows how God would vote in a political election. The believer, it is asserted, has no choice, and this then defines the social life of the church.

Not all congregants were pleased. One woman in suburban Atlanta expressed her dismay in a series of e-mail messages to the editors of *Religion in the News:*

> The "in crowd" at my church is all Republican and regularly encouraged others in the church to attend the Christian Coalition meetings and rallies. They also ask for volunteers to help them in the election campaigns of Republican candidates. The Deacons and Pastor invite Republican candidates to come to speak at our church, but never invite Democrats.
>
> In all meals or meetings in the Church Fellowship Hall, whenever talk turns to politics and current affairs, the Church leaders always point out that the Republican Party is the one that represents "Christian values" and "Christian people" should always support them. . . . Whenever I tried to point out church is not the appropriate place for secular politics, I always been pooh-poohed.
>
> Sunday morning before an election day, the so-called Christian Coalition Voter Guide is distributed in the vestibule of my church (and hundreds of others across the state). The preacher always makes an announcement about it and exhorts everyone to be sure to pick one up as they leave the sanctuary. There is always a stack of these "voters guides" (which amount to Republican tickets) left in the vestibule, easily available to voters when they come to vote on Tuesday.[11]

People were interacting with each other on matters of political concern, and the consequences of their interactions were politically significant. They acted together and voted Republican. They acted together and got out the vote. They acted together and demonstrated for issues of common concern, against "the homosexual agenda," for "family values," against abortion, for the war on terrorism, and so forth. And they did so with the guidance of their ministers, which presented problems.

On the question of separation of church and state, the minister activists were prepared. The fundamentalist National Clergy Council's approach presented the general strategy. It sought to educate all its members about the key issues of abortion, homosexual marriage, and the role of God in American society. It assumed in the words of its president, Reverend Rob Schenck, that "pastors hold a very high place of respect in the eyes of their congregants" and that "the pastor has an enormous influence on the thinking of the members of his congregation." The council's project was to have pastors focus in their church activities on key moral issues of life, marriage, and God in America. This was the position of President Bush and the Republican Party. But Schenck maintained that the pastor supported the message not politically but in terms of "a moral and spiritual reformation." His group provided methods to draw this fine line. According to Schenck, "It is not liberal or conservative that matters, what matters are the core issues that are involved with the Gospel and with Christian moral teachings." The group was not partisan in its activities, Schenck argued: "Whether one party comes out on top or the other is a non-issue. . . . What we hope and pray is that the right moral and spiritual outcomes will result from the elections. It's up to the parties themselves to decide whether they want to be part of that moral and spiritual reformation." That the group and its clergy membership, and many other religious leaders of the Christian right consistently supported Republicans and President Bush was accordingly maintained to be secondary. Primary was the pursuit of their religious mission.[12]

This may or may not have been constitutional, from the point of view of the courts. It may or may not violate statutory restrictions on tax-exempt organizations according to the IRS. It was, nonetheless, used by political strategists to win the presidential election. The Bush-Cheney reelection campaign developed a detailed plan to capture and mobilize the support of evangelical Christians. It asked churches for directories of their members, distributed issue guides in churches, and urged pastors to hold voter-registration drives.[13]

Thus the face-to-face interactions in churches were embedded in a system of support and coordination. Social movements such as the Christian Coalition tried to mobilize individual and group support for their specific religious and political agenda. This agenda was primarily articulated in churches by local religious leaders. The political project of supporting specific politicians was interpreted as being a religious and moral one. This interpretation became the basis of interaction in the churches. Political debate ended and religious mandate was invoked. And this religious mandate was used to mobilize voters by political operatives, such as those in the Bush-Cheney reelection campaign.

Those on the religious right did work in their local churches and talk to each other about a common set of pressing political concerns. They used the churches for political means. They acted on a small scale, and their actions had large consequences. Some in these churches and many in the greater society were concerned that this undermined the constitutional principle of the separation of church and state. Nonetheless, political power was generated by small interactions.

The greatest immediate significance of these interactions on the right was that they matched and perhaps surpassed the mobilization capacity of the left. There was a high turnout on election day, and despite the commonsense assumption that this would be to the advantage of the Democrats, the Republicans prevailed, retaining control of Congress and the White House. But this immediate victory overshadowed a potentially significant long-term consequence of the local mobilizations in the churches. Through their connections to the broader mobilizations of the Republican Party and conservative social movements, they have changed political discussion in the United States: they have given voice to the religious right on cultural matters, from the hot campaign issues of abortion and gay marriage to the issues of broadcasting decency and the inclusion of a religious sensibility in public life. Christian conservatives, along with other conservatives, have articulated a concern about such matters and have put them on the public agenda with great success.

Politics or Power?

Talk is not always cheap. Sometimes it is very consequential. New voices were articulated more clearly on both the left and the right in 2004, but whether these voices contributed to a democratic dialogue or democratic outcomes was not at all certain. Dialogue is a key to the notion of free politics as formulated by Arendt and as applied in this study. In a democratic dialogue, people come together as equals. They speak and act in each other's presence and develop the capacity to act in concert on the basis of their interactions. Informed discussion is central to a democratic politics, the basis of democratic political power.[14] We saw in chapters 2 and 3 how this power was generated and how it changed the political landscape in the former Soviet bloc. Dialogue there generated enough power, first, to challenge the totalitarian order, then, in the long run, to support democratic outcomes. The capacity to act together was the basis of the power, the openness of the dialogue a key to its democratic quality. In 2004 the power of the politics of small things was again evident, refuting the ignorance of 2001, but its democratic quality needs critical appraisal. This is apparent in the very constitution of these politics as they appear on the right and as they are manifested across the political spectrum.

In the churches, the small interactions were not based in equality. Or at least, some there were definitely more equal then others. The authoritative capacity of the pastors to speak on religious issues was transferred to political discussion. This may not be all that different, however, from the development of hierarchy in most human endeavors, particularly political ones. The Dean candidacy may have been more a manifestation of small virtual egalitarian interactions, but the interactions were first constituted by the most politically active and technologically advanced. Bloggers and the founders of MoveOn.net and Meetup.com, in particular, had greater authority and power. And once the interactions led to the development of political leadership, which enabled the movement to say more than no to the dominant authorities, new authorities were created. The voice of a Howard Dean or a Joe Trippi, the chair of Dean's campaign, certainly had greater authority in the movement than those of ordinary activists. At the meet-up described in chapter 5, there were organizers who had regular contacts with and influence on campaign officials that other participants did not have. While people in religious congregations who met and acted together politically were guided by the existing hierarchies of their communities, people who met on the Internet and in meet-ups were guided by an emerging hierarchy. From the point of view of a critical thinker, such as Michel Foucault, these hierarchies may be of crucial importance. Enactment of power more than dialogic interaction would be seen as being constitutive of the social situation.

As was the case with the snapshots of the democratic opposition in Poland presented in chapter 1, both the virtual politics of small things, as seen in the antiwar movement and the Dean campaign, and the mobilization of the religious right are open to competing interpretations. It is clear that small things matter. Among the Deaniacs and the antiwar activists, as among Christian conservatives, micropolitics made a difference. How we judge them is another matter.

In the accounts of the snapshots of the Polish opposition, the contrast between an Arendt-Goffman interpretation and a Foucaultian interpretation did not revolve around the importance of the kitchen table, the bookstore, or the literary salon. The issue was how, within each of these situations, truth was related to power, whether a distinction could be made between the relationship in these settings and in official interactions. Foucault knew that micropolitics are significant. This is why he studied "sovereignty with the king's head cut off." The question is whether a distinction can be made between the micropolitics of the powers and their alternatives, whether the alternatives merely involve a new truth regime that cannot be qualitatively distinguished from the old regime. From Foucault's point of view, as we have seen, the official interactions that produced new socialist men cannot be critically distinguished from the ones I was remembering, in which the rules of officialdom were suspended and people interacted with each other by, as Havel put it, "living in truth."

The perspective of Arendt and Goffman provided a way to make this distinction. At issue, for Arendt, is the conflicted relation between truth and politics. She highlighted two important components of the relationship, the need to base a sound politics on factual truth and the need to distinguish political opinion from truth. A politics that substitutes fabrication for factual truth cannot provide the grounds for a sound politics, and a political position that asserts that a particular political opinion is the truth allows no room for political life. We know that drawing distinctions between philosophical truth and factual truth is not easy, but it is in human interaction that such distinctions are pursued. This Goffman illuminates. The snapshots presented in chapter 1 revealed people in their interactions making these distinctions, as they redefined the situations in which they acted. From this perspective the "truth regime" of the postcommunist social order was qualitatively different from that of the previously existing communist one. In the postcommunist order there was an attempt to base politics on a factual truth and to keep politics open to the confrontation of different opinions. Under the communists such factual basis and openness were neither pursued nor permitted. The weakness of Foucault's position is that he cannot make this distinction.

Yet this does not mean that Foucault is completely wrong. The sort of relation that he sees between knowledge and power does exist, and there are often tendencies in this direction. Both Arendt and Goffman recognize this, she in her studies of totalitarianism, he in his analysis of total institutions. This relationship is a part of social life, just not necessarily all of it.

In the interactions among antiwar and Dean bloggers, there were some issues that were a matter of opinion but were treated as truth. The bloggers were open to different opinions about how to oppose George W. Bush, but support for Bush's policies was not permitted. When contributors to threads on the elections were openly critical of the Democrats and supportive of Bush, they were denounced as "trolls," and their postings were often deleted. Some opinions were just not acceptable. Perhaps this was not an instance of an official truth, but it did restrict dialogue. This is what critics observed when they noted that there seemed to be a balkanization of political life. Political address had become a means to preach to the converted.

But the restrictions among Deaniacs and antiwar activists pale next to the situation among the Christian conservatives. Among these conservatives preaching to the converted, or the born again, replaced politicking as a matter of principle. The truth was more directly the opponent of politics. Opinion was tightly closed. Political position was defined by religious truth. Ironically, when representatives of the Christian right argued for its political neutrality, they themselves emphasized this aspect of their approach to politics, as we have seen. They in effect argued, when explaining why they did not violate tax laws that prohibit religious institutions from engaging in politics, that theirs was a project in which religious truth trumped politics. In supporting Republican candidates, they were following religious principles, not engaging in partisan politics. The alternatives they presented emerged not from a free politics of small things but from a common commitment to religious revelation. This contributed to an electoral victory, but it unsettles democratic practices.

This judgment of the politics of the Christian right is certainly a political one, I recognize. But it is based on theoretical insight and not only partisanship. I am concerned, perhaps more than many Americans, about the infusion of religious rhetoric in American public life. On the central political stage, the declared war against the axis of evil seems to me to resemble too closely the fundamentalism of the new totalitarians of religious revelation. The politics of the Christian right, off center stage, as it mobilized support for Republican candidates and the Republican Party, likewise substituted religious truth for political opinion. Although those who were involved acted because of conviction and not because of coercion, their actions, nonetheless, weakened an independent politics even as they created an electoral power that has changed the political map. Small things do matter. They were effective. But in Arendt's sense, their actions were not political. They were more like the micropolitics of Foucault than the politics of small things informed by the political theory of Arendt.

A note of clarification: I am not asserting that to connect any religious sensibility or insight to politics is undemocratic. The problem arises in the way they are connected, in the substitution of one for the other. The problem parallels the politics identified with science, or pseudoscience, that were prominent in the last century. Not only did the ideologies of race and class inform Soviet and Nazi totalitarian practices, but expert knowledge replaced politics in governance of the technocratic welfare state. Science was not the issue; rather it was the substitution of scientific or scientistic decisions for political ones.

In the twenty-first century, the truth that seems to be most directly challenging democracy is religious. It is not religion, or its truth as such, that presents the challenge. When religion informs political dialogue but does not determine the outcome of the dialogue, democracy can proceed and even be strengthened. This Tocqueville observed when considering democracy in America in the nineteenth century. People form judgments about the problems of the day based on their most fundamental beliefs and act accordingly in the public sphere. There is still a free exchange of alternative opinions in a pluralistic society based on a multiplicity of beliefs. But when particular beliefs are presented as definitively deciding controversial issues of public concern and people act to prevail on the basis of the beliefs' truth, religion has been substituted for free political interaction. This Tocqueville also observed.[15] Theocracy, or at least theocratic conflict, then replaces democracy. Religious mandate, rather than political interaction, is seen as decisive. This is a primary danger in our times, as the central political stage is occupied by the crusade against Islamic terror, and it is a serious threat to the politics of small things.

The Small Political Landscape in the Shadows

In 2004, the political game was radically changed in America. The politics of small things, manifested through new technologies, presented a new force with potentially enduring effects. The importance of the micropolitics of the religious right also had great consequences. These two forces were in partisan conflict. The right prevailed. But more important than this is how the two forces have reshaped the American political landscape. After the attacks of September 11, 2001, the declaration of a war on terrorism, and the military conflicts in Afghanistan and Iraq, a new kind of politics is emerging. Alternatives have been articulated through this politics. New forms of democratic and undemocratic action have been presented. And the struggle for democratic alternatives is ongoing. We saw in the last chapter how the politics of small things has presented alternatives to the big politics of the global stage. We have seen in this chapter how this political alternative must work against not only actions on the big stage, but also interactions on small localized ones. This work involves social movements pitted against each other and responding to large-scale political, military, and cultural actions, from the workings of political parties to the workings of armies and the development of religious movements. But it also must involve more stable settings in social institutions, to which we now turn.

7

Institutions: Democracy in the Details

July 10, 2002. "Debbie," a human rights activist from Burma, proudly introduces herself to my class in Cracow, Poland, as a threat to national security: her commitment to democratic values has put her so at odds with two Southeast Asian governments that she must travel clandestinely using a nom de guerre. Yet as our seminar on democratic culture comes to an end, she, of all people, declares: "I have doubted a simple assertion for years, but I am now convinced that American democracy requires the repression of democracy in the rest of the world." Quite provocatively, she is expressing the consensus of the students in the seminar. These young people, moved by values of human rights and democracy, have also become convinced that the existence of these rights in America is predicated on their repression elsewhere. If ever there was an indication of the failure of the American war on terrorism, this is it. The militarized response to the threat of terror had turned democrats from elsewhere into skeptics and enemies of American policies, even before the war in Iraq.

Every January I travel to Cape Town, South Africa, to teach in a program on democracy and diversity. Every July I travel to Cracow to teach in a parallel program. Advanced graduate students, professors, human rights activists, and young public policy advisors are brought together by the Transregional Center for Democratic Studies of the New

School. The program has its origins in the Democracy Seminar, a clandestine intellectual exchange between Budapest, Warsaw, and New York in the 1980s, organized by Adam Michnik and me.[1] The seminar, that is, was a product of the politics of small things in the old bloc. Democratic oppositionists and New School scholars became colleagues as they read and discussed classics in political theory and the pressing problems of the day. The students attending our seminars—from southern Africa, Eastern and Central Europe, the nations of the former Soviet Union, Southeast Asia, and North and South America—continue this discussion.

What I observed among these young opinion leaders in January 2002 in Africa, and later that year in Central Europe, was striking. Anti-Americanism revealed itself not just as a hysterical judgment popular on the political fringe. It had become a principle of committed democrats, and this, unfortunately, made a great deal of sense when it came to the war on terrorism.

In the Cape Town seminar, we started our deliberations with reflections on the September 11 attacks. I was surprised by the classroom discussion. With the exception of one young professor from Nigeria, all the students were focused not on confronting al Qaeda but on the American war on terrorism. It seemed that the participants could not imagine that the Americans were victims. They could only understand our power and condemn our excesses.

Whereas I understood the American operation in Afghanistan as fundamentally a liberation, my South African coteacher and our students understood it as superpower bullying. Whereas I wanted to understand the mind-set of those who would kill thousands of innocents, including one of my dearest friends, in a suicide bombing, they could only see the horrors of collateral damage of the war on terrorism.

In Cracow I waited until the end of the seminar to open the discussion to September 11 and its aftermath. Before September 11, anti-Americanism in Europe was a mild affair and a key part of the love-hate relationship between the French and the Americans. In the aftermath of the attacks and with the war on terrorism in full swing, it could not have been more serious.

One of the students explained why they needed to focus on the reaction to the attacks and not the attacks themselves. The war on terrorism was being used as cover by dictators around the world to justify crackdowns on democracy advocates. Suddenly the rights of Muslims in the Philippines and Indonesia—and of democratic critics of the authoritarian "Asian way" in Singapore, Malaysia, and Burma—were not important to the Bush administration. Suddenly the strategic resources of central Asian dictatorships were more important than the lives of human rights activists. Suddenly defense of the American way of life and our democracy seemed to be predicated upon a lack of concern for the democratic rights of people in less advantaged countries.

As a rule, in my judgment, American democracy does not depend on the frustration of democratic prospects in the rest of the world. All too often this does seem to be the case, but at other times the United States has played crucial roles in supporting democratic activists, as it did in Poland. But the fact remains, official policy did make the struggle for democracy a secondary priority in American geopolitical calculations during the cold war, and in the aftermath of the attacks of September 11, 2001, this has happened again.

When I think about my students, it seems to me that the young Muslim from Indonesia, the Burmese dissident living in Thailand, the democrat returning to Burma, and the feminists in Poland, Ukraine, Slovakia, the Czech Republic, and Indonesia are the keys to victory against dogmatism and its terrors. Only they are actually capable of presenting alternatives to terrorism to their compatriots; that work cannot be done from afar. They are on the front lines of the antiterrorist struggle. Any war that undermines their position—and they convincingly report that it is doing so—is self-defeating. In other words, I am convinced that their politics of small things is an essential element in the global struggle against terrorism. In fact, I believe that their political struggles are intimately connected with ours, and that the antiwar movement and the Dean campaign, as I attempted to show in chapter 5, effectively made this connection through a virtually organized politics of small things.

Yet, while it is important to recognize the achievements of the antiwar movement and the Dean campaign as social movements, and to understand their grounding in the politics of small things and their connections to such politics around the world, it is also important to recognize the limitations of those movements and the challenges to the politics of small things within social movements. Fluid movements do yield important political and cultural changes, but they have a tendency to disappear as rapidly as they appear. The power of the definition of the situation is unstable when it is not institutionalized. The Dean campaign, MoveOn.com, and the antiwar movement presented a clear and negative evaluation of official American policy in the war on terrorism and in the pursuit of neoliberal domestic policies. They confronted the mobilization of the religious right. Ultimately they did not prevail. Still, an ongoing alternative will be presented to the American people when it is institutionalized within one of the two dominant political parties. The institutionalization of the politics of small things is a key to the long-term viability of such politics.

And such institutionalization is possible not only in political parties. In fact, it can be and is achieved in a broad range of social institutions. Educational institutions and media institutions, as we will observe, are particularly important. It is in such locations that the power of a sacralized politics can be addressed, not in a partisan way but as a matter of democratic principles.

Established social institutions are locations of interactive improvisation for political and social creativity. The struggle over social definition is often a regular part of their everyday life. This is true even in societies directed and controlled by totalitarian parties, and it is a normal aspect of everyday life in liberal democratic social orders. The politics of small things often begin in institutions, and it is in institutions that the political project of small things is realized. Frequently the struggle over definition centers on relatively mundane matters not directly connected to the central problems of the day, but if we are to find alternatives to new totalized temptations, and to new threats "the truth" poses to a free political life, we should pay close attention. Doing so requires an understanding of the multidimensional qualities of everyday life and the struggles of establishing different frameworks within which the situation may be defined. This was starkly evident around the old Soviet bloc.

The Politics of Small Things in Social Institutions
before the Fall of Communism

Outsiders observing the communist system ranked the various regimes along a continuum, from hard-line to liberal, according to the prevailing party line. In Central Europe, Hungary and Poland were generally understood to be liberal, while Czechoslovakia and Romania were considered more hard-line. Although there was something to this way of viewing things—the range of unorthodox activities publicly evident in these countries did follow this pattern—there is still something one-dimensional about this account. The political culture in each of the countries was constituted by an ongoing conflict, built into the life of the society. The party line was one factor. The other was the social response to the party line, in ordinary moments as well as extraordinary ones. The conflict was most apparent in 1968 and in the struggles leading up to the great transformations of 1989, as we have already observed. The people challenging party restrictions in Poland were the ones who opened Polish society, not the party apparatchiks who tried to control them. In

Czechoslovakia, on the other hand, the liberal leadership played a greater role than did popular challenges.

In all spheres of life, a social, interactive contesting of the definition of the situation was evident. In educational institutions, arts institutions, industrial and communication institutions, there was an ongoing struggle between those who enforced the dominant order of things and those who challenged it. The interaction between the censor and the censored, the archetype of this sort of thing, indicates repression, but it also indicates a persistent challenging of repression. The challenge became historically significant with the development of the politics of small things as a sustained alternative force, when people began to coordinate their actions. The case of the Academy of Movement, analyzed in chapter 3, was a slightly comic version of these concerted efforts in everyday life.

This is not as exotic as it may seem. Within all social and cultural institutions there is an interaction that at its core is political. Institutions discipline, as Michel Foucault emphasizes, but they also present the context for creativity and autonomy. The tension between these functions provides a central domain for the politics of small things. Consider how the politics of small things play out in two significant cultural institutions, education and the mass media, both of which are crucial for understanding the small alternatives to terrorism and militarized antiterrorism and to sacralized politics.

Education

The seminar was about democracy in America. It was a first-year seminar designed to accomplish two things. It provided a group of students the opportunity to read one of the classics, Alexis de Tocqueville's *Democracy in America,* and it guided the students in their educational journey from high school learning to the more reflective inquiry of an American liberal arts education. It was a place for discipline. It was a place for freedom. It had a difficult relationship with politics and with vocation.

When the participants of the seminar first gathered, the rules of the game were established. The substantive elements were straightforward, summarized in the syllabus and in my overview of the assignments. I had taught this course before; providing an overview of the academic tasks was a simple matter. But turning a meeting of first-year students studying a subject they deeply cared about into a real educational setting was another matter. The challenge facing the students and me was at first primarily an expressive one. They had to show me that they were interested. I had to reveal to them that it mattered.

I explained that Tocqueville was a nineteenth century political pilgrim who came to the United States to see the future, and who wrote a two-volume work that was both a description of the ways of the Americans, their society, and their system of governance and a sociological theory of democratic society. I told them that at times Tocqueville would seem to be writing about the Americans but was really reflecting upon democrats, while at other times he addressed the characteristics of democracy and was actually writing about America. He identified the notion of a democratic society with that of American society, even confused them.

I posed a question to the students: How would they identify American society? Free, imperialist, capitalist, selfish, and reactionary were among their responses. The political consensus of the student body at Eugene Lang College is far to the left of the American political consensus, even to the left of the American academic consensus. These were young radicals, bohemians drawn to a progressive liberal arts college in lower Manhattan. We would have many interesting political discussions in the classroom, which was very much my intention. But we had to work together to maintain the classroom as both an educational setting and a place where individual judgment could be passionately expressed. We had to define the situation.

The ideas of Tocqueville could not be more important for me. In fact, his understanding of the need to investigate the mores of American society and its associational practices provide a starting point for understanding the institutional settings of the politics of small things. If I had to choose a nineteenth-century thinker to provide a guide for the problems of the twenty-first century, Tocqueville would be my choice. There are a variety of reasons for this. He explored the underside of modern democracy before much of it had happened. He appreciated the importance of nonpolitical institutions and movements as a way of avoiding that underside. His position on political matters transcends political clichés. He is equally appealing to the liberal, the conservative, and the radical. He saw democracy as something that is always in play. I explained this to the class, as I suggested to them that many of their characterizations, the negative and the positive, are a result of the democratic character of American society.

I highlighted Tocqueville's project in an attempt to show them that understanding democracy in America, both then and now, is a complicated business, worthy of our serious engagement. We had to work together to establish our gathering as a genuine educational setting, and this required presentational work. I had to speak with confidence, be engaging, demonstrate excitement and passion about the subject. They had to appear to pay attention and appear to be interested. Sometimes when I worked on the appearance of my engagement, I might have worked to the point that I lost track of what exactly I was trying to appear engaged with. And they, with their expressions of interest and involvement with my presentation, also would sometimes work so hard that they did not hear or understand exactly what I was saying. I know this because reflecting on the construction of the definition of the situation in the seminar classroom is something that I always share with my classes. When they answered questions or asked their own, the same dynamic would be present. They would defer to my authority and my demeanor would embody it, while I would also understate the assertion of authority, through my tone of address, body carriage, and eye contact to indicate openness to later discussions. These patterns of deference and demeanor contributed to the character of our class. They indicated a specific definition of a learning situation.

This is how the rules of the interactive game of a seminar are constituted. Reading and writing assignments, required oral presentations, and class participation establish an organizational framework, which is embedded within broader college and university parameters and the interactions between educational institutions and the greater society. But the participants define the life of the seminar through their interactions. When a professor comes in with yellowing notes and mechanically gets through them, and when students nod off in response, no matter how excellent the institution of higher learning, no matter how brilliant the students and the professor, the class ends in failure. My students and I worked in our opening sessions to define our seminar as a real place of learning, a place where alternative points of view would be expressed and evidence and quality of argumentation respected. And because we defined it as such, there was a greatly increased possibility for it to be so.

At stake was not just one class, at one college, for one group of students and their professor. Rather the very nature of higher learning was being worked on. We had it in our power to decide on major issues in the culture wars, on the relation between politics and education, general and vocational education, discipline and autonomy.

To begin with, I was at odds with the students about the relation between politics and education. In a class of fifteen only one could be described as in any way right of center. Most of the students were young radicals, highly critical of the American way of life, though a centrist or two were also present. The majority had a fresh youthful disdain and suspicion of the ruling powers as they understood them, a prematurely jaded view of American values. As an expert in modern tyranny, I feel that they do need to distinguish the failures of liberalism from the principles of totalitarianism. But I do not take convincing students of my political position to be my role in the classroom. Rather, it is to open them up to considering alternative judgments, while their role is to learn more about the world they inhabit and will be responsible for. This is a small but important political matter. These practices were directed toward opening a space for education. They had broad political significance, although they were not connected with a specific political (partisan) position.

On the political right and left, the classroom is understood as a major political battlefield. The neo, and not so neo, conservatives view the classroom as a place to provide students with an understanding of the great achievements of "our" civilization. Progressives view the classroom as a place to provide critiques of this civilization and to reveal the evils of Western hegemony. My students were attracted to Eugene Lang College because it presents itself as being a progressive educational institution, in contrast to conservative, more conventional institutions, as in fact does the New School as a whole. Yet I believe that this is a mistaken way of understanding our institution and tried to demonstrate this to them both as part of a specific argument about politics and education and by showing them the benefits of my position for the life of our seminar.

It is my position that politics has to be set apart from education in the university just as religion has to be set apart from politics in churches, in both cases for the good of both the specific cultural endeavor, the church or the university, and the broader political one. I believe that learning and teaching constitute the free public space in education, and these practices have a very difficult relationship to politics. Addressing this difficult relationship is a way of confronting the sort of problems that are now arising on the American scene regarding the relation between religion and politics; it is important to understand that they are not unrelated but that they must be connected and separated very carefully. Ideally this is an important part of the educational enterprise.

Although education may be about politics, it should be distanced from the central political stage. In fact, partisan politics compromises education, and education compromises politics in crucial ways. This suggests that there is something very wrong with the positions taken in the American cultural wars of the past decades. I think we should understand what conservatives and radicals contribute to the project of education, while we distance ourselves from their partisan positions (even those we share outside the classroom). In the classroom, the positions should be understood as existing in dialogue, without easy prefabricated conclusions.

Politics and education should be set at a distance from each other, or the ideals of both will be compromised.

Education as a problem in politics. The modern tyrant tries to educate the population, to build Soviet Man or, as in Pinochet's Chile and other authoritarian political orders, to prepare the nation for democracy. Hannah Arendt observes the general principle: "Education can play no part in [free] politics, because in politics we always have to deal with those who are already educated. Whoever wants to educate adults really wants to act as their guardian and prevent them from political activity."[2] Confusing education with politics substitutes the authoritative relationship between teacher and students for the democratic relationship among citizens.

Politics as a problem of education. On the other hand, the substitution of a citizen's relationship for the relationship between teacher and student is also a problem. It undermines the educational endeavor. Students have to be prepared to take part in the world, but they are not yet equipped to do so. The educator's first responsibility to her or his students is to present them with the world as he or she knows it, so that they can later act upon it, based on their own judgments. Students must be protected from immediate political and economic concerns and pressures, so that they can be prepared to take part in public life as mature, responsible, equal citizens. Along these lines, Michael Oakeshott observes, "Education in its most general significance may be recognized as a specific transaction which may go on between generations of human beings in which newcomers to the scene are initiated into the world they are to inhabit."[3] He explains that a liberal education involves "the invitation to disentangle oneself, for a time, from the urgencies of the here and now and to listen to the conversation in which human beings forever seek to understand themselves."[4] Oakeshott succinctly tells us what education is in its most basic sense, a transaction between one generation and the next, and specifies the particulars of a liberal education.[5] It is free and directed toward understanding the human condition. The dynamic keyword in this basic approach to education is "conversation." Oakeshott understands conversation to be the operative element of liberal education, underscoring that it must be conducted freely, unconstrained by either the powers that be or their critics. I agree. Education is a special kind of free public activity. The politics of small things within an educational enterprise is about providing space for such activity.

So the first problem of the seminar, from my point of view, was to create for the students a context for a conversation about the human condition. It could be achieved only as an interactive enterprise, which I see as grounded in a position combining Goffman's and Arendt's understandings of the constitution of public life.

At first we did not know each other, and a clear definition of the rules of the seminar game had not yet been established. A social etiquette was established, very much guided by me, the professor. The seminar was to be a gathering of equals, with each participant's voice taken seriously. The quality of their arguments and judgments would of course be critically evaluated by the group, but no view could be simply dismissed or accepted. I then presented the class with its first expressive challenge: to make room for responsible alternative positions. When a Cuban American student defined the United States in our first meeting in terms that were, for this group, unusually positive, the other students, with my guidance, reacted respectfully. This anticipated future respectful discussions, on much more difficult issues. In a protest against the American military intervention in Iraq, students occupied the office of the university president, Bob Kerrey, a vocal proponent of intervention. One of the students in my seminar took part in the action, while another was a strong supporter of U.S. actions. They had no problem talking about this and other controversial issues in the class as they illuminated Tocqueville on America and democracy. When the prowar student was reluctant to explain her position fully, the student radicals encouraged her to share her judgments. The students actually came to seek out their differences in order to understand each other.

Perhaps in retrospect, my memory of this seminar is colored by nostalgia for a job well done and an appreciation for an admirable group of young people. But even if this is so, the memory points to an important dimension of the forces in play in a learning situation. We were engaged in the constitution of a liberal arts inquiry in Oakeshott's sense, rejecting political definitions of education, those of both the left and the right, and vocational definitions, and we did this by developing an anti-ideological reading of *Democracy in America*.

A college education is a way to appreciate the great accomplishments of "our civilization," and it is a way to question Western history, and it is a way to get a good job. All these expectations promote views of education as an instrument to some extraeducational purpose, political or economic, and all operate in the classroom as a part of the everyday life of higher education. Nonetheless, in the classroom an alternative to such disciplining of the educational project is a possibility—but only if the participants, the teachers and students, define it as such. It is the fruit of the politics of small things. It is not a partisan politics, but a politics concerned with autonomy, with self-definition, and as such it prepares the students and the teachers to conduct themselves beyond the classroom in the larger political arena.

We observed this same public quality around the kitchen table, in the clandestine bookstore, and at the illegal poetry reading in Poland. In each of those cases, the possibility of independent action was built from within the fabric of everyday life. This is exactly what did not happen in the churches mobilized by the religious right. In the classroom, it is independent judgment, a central goal of a liberal education, that is being cultivated. Reproducing the traditional task of a liberal education requires the work of students and teachers.

Things get more explicitly political when we turn our attention to the mass media.

The Media

Journalism is a cultural institution that is surrounded by controversy. Are the media tools of the left or right? Does journalism function as the fourth estate, a critical branch of democratic governance? Or is it a servant of the powers? When we look closely, we will observe that these are questions answered in the details. It matters how journalists conduct their jobs and how they together develop an understanding of their responsibilities. By the way they conduct their activities together journalists, like the participants in a college seminar or in evangelical churches, shape the nature of their cultural institution. The functional needs of the powers and the development of adversary culture surround media journalists, as Chomsky and Goldberg highlight.[6] Yet the way media journalists relate to the public, as I argued in opening this inquiry, depends upon not only such large structures but also the interactive understandings journalists have of their profession. Consider a case in the 1990s when real innovation was constituted by practicing journalists and their associates. It started with the presidential campaign of 1988.

During that campaign, political rhetoric reached new cynical heights in America. Responsibility for this dubious achievement most directly should be placed with the political actors involved, the makers of the Republican and Democratic campaigns. Yet journalists and others in the news media asked the reflective question about their own involvement. There was an understanding, broadly shared by the movers and shakers in the American world of journalism, that prevailing journalistic practices fed public cynicism.[7] The cynicism was most frontally expressed when the Republican presidential candidate, George H. W. Bush, made his infamous promise not to raise taxes, articulated with the emotional power of a Clint Eastwood: "Read my lips, no new taxes!" At that time, it was clear that some sort of revenue enhancement, as taxes were then euphemistically called, would be necessary to control the ballooning deficit and to cover federal spending. Almost all responsible economists agreed with this necessity. But Bush made an impossible political promise the cornerstone of his successful bid for the presidency, which he broke once elected. His opponent, Michael Dukakis, indicated his opposition to tax hikes but would not rule them out in such categorical and forceful terms. The forcefulness of Bush's promise, carefully packaged by his campaign team in political ads and in sound bites for television and radio broadcast, turned a vote for the Republican ticket into a vote against taxes and a vote for the Democratic ticket into a vote for taxes.

The news media reported these exchanges and strategies, along with such equally elevated issues as Dukakis's unwillingness to support an amendment to the Constitution to ban the burning of the American flag. The general approach of the media was to report the claims and counterclaims of the two parties and to assess how well the claims were received by the electorate. In this way, the media amplified the political cynicism. They made accounts of the effectiveness of cynical political strategies the primary story line of their campaign reporting. Few reports included analysis of the significant differences in actual policy positions of the two major candidates. The campaign was not about the fundamental problems facing American society at the close of the twentieth century: the radical changes in the relationship with the Soviet Union and the changing world economic system, with all the implications of those changes for the American citizenry. Instead cynicism and silly campaign gimmicks dominated accounts of the political process. Many journalists were critically aware of this.

The prevailing press response to the problem of cynicism in political campaigns was to attempt to get to the truth of what was thought to be behind political campaign promises and attacks. The careful review of political advertising, for example, became a standard feature of newspaper and broadcast reporting. Public claims by political figures were carefully scrutinized. But this had obvious drawbacks. The story line was still defined by the political contest and its ability to draw the attention of a large audience, which may or may not have been directed to public concerns and a care for the constitution of a public space for deliberation. The advocates of major journalism reform understood that constituting this space was crucially important. They were concerned that political reporting had become a sort of sports reporting, presenting accounts of who was winning and who was losing, using all the complicated appara-

tus of public opinion polling and focus groups. Politicians use this apparatus to plot political strategy, to direct campaigns; media analysts use the
same apparatus to report on the strategies and the campaigns.

"Public journalism" or "civic journalism," as it is variously named,
was developed as a critical response to this and involved innovations in
journalistic ethics and practices. Those involved in this movement realized that there has been a deliberation deficit in American society.[8] News-
gathering following conventional formulas, they understood, would not
solve the problems. Public journalism was a movement of journalists and
academics, supported by some foundations and corporations, that argued that the journalist has a responsibility to report and analyze news
in a way that contributes to pubic enlightenment and addresses public
problems, not simply to report objectively.

One of the most forceful advocates of this approach to journalism was
Davis (Buzz) Merritt, the editor of the *Wichita Eagle* of Wichita, Kansas.
In an editorial in his newspaper, he explained his paper's mode of reporting to its readers by citing the debate between John Dewey and Walter
Lippmann on the public as it occurred in the 1920s.[9] He stressed that in
this famous debate between America's leading columnist and leading
public philosopher, the columnist, Lippmann, argued for an elitist position: that the general public was not capable of understanding the complicated issues of the day, that they should be shielded from policy discussions in their complications, that their decisions should be limited to
approval or disapproval of those in power. Merritt underscored that this
position has prevailed in American journalistic practices. He argued that
public journalism should be informed by the more democratic position of
Dewey. It should try to bridge the gap between the political class and the
rest of the population, rather than viewing it as inevitable, seeking to include the citizenry into the deliberations and actions of public life, not
simply presenting public life as a spectator sport to a passive audience.

This was the primary thrust of public journalism. It attempted to
bring the public back into the journalistic and the political enterprise. It
viewed its readers, listeners, and viewers not only as an audience to be
marketed to, but as a public to be engaged. And it was not just a fuzzy-
minded utopian movement of the academic elite. It had a clear economic
rationale. It was conceived not just as an alternative on the political
fringes but as a fiscally sound strategy for communication corporations,
with a pluralistic political approach. Let me give you some examples.

The *Bradenton Herald* of Bradenton, Florida, in 1994, took an unusual
step when it was announced that the local superintendent of schools was
retiring.[10] It sought to ensure that the public played a role in finding a

successor. This relatively small newspaper sent its reporters to local voluntary associations, church groups, parent teacher associations, and other local public gatherings. They discovered that the people of the community, when asked, expressed an interest in changing the leadership of the school system. The paper then invited various citizens to speak with its editorial board. As a result of the discussion there, the school board was inspired to launch a national search for the open position instead of accepting the recommendation of the retiring superintendent. The newspaper's creation of a public discussion created political pressure. It made it possible for citizens to speak and act in each other's presence and to create power based on the politics of small things. The newspaper's offices began to function as a sort of review panel to help screen the candidates. The paper even sent reporters to the candidates' hometowns to report on their qualifications. The *Bradenton Herald* transformed itself into an active reporting forum for the consideration of a pressing public issue and guided action based upon the results of the forum. It, in effect, created a local social movement for educational reform.

Similarly, but on a much broader public stage, a group of newspapers and television and radio stations in North Carolina applied the public journalism concept to coverage of the political campaign in 1996.[11] This was especially significant because Jesse Helms, the archconservative senator and head of the Senate Foreign Affairs Committee, was campaigning for reelection. The race was a replay of the 1990 contest between Helms and Harvey Gantt, a moderate Democrat with political positions more or less similar to those of Bill Clinton. Gantt, as the cliché goes, happens to be African American. He was running against the most conservative member of the U.S. Senate to be the first black senator from the old Confederacy since Reconstruction. In the 1990 election, Helms had used explicitly racist themes to narrowly prevail. The election had little to do with the pressing issues of the day other than those of race as it was manifested in charges and countercharges concerning affirmative action and its threat to "equal rights for whites."

With this past experience in mind, fifteen media organizations, including six newspapers, five commercial television stations, three radio stations, and the state's public television channel, formed the "Your Voice, Your Vote" consortium. This media group commissioned two public opinion surveys: one for the primary season in January and the other during the general election in July. These polls sought to discern which issues the public judged to be of pressing concern. The group analyzed the results to inform how it would cover the elections. It determined that for the general election four distinct issues were of paramount importance to the public: crime and drugs, taxes and spending, affordable health care, and education. The group then invited all the candidates for governor and senator, the two major contested statewide offices, for intensive three-hour videotaped interviews. These became the basis of independently published and broadcast stories in each of the news outlets. The interviews and the polls also were used as the starting point for subsequent coverage of the campaign as it progressed.

The result of this major exercise in public journalism was campaign coverage that was markedly more serious and less sensational than is the American norm. But there were significant problems. Helms refused to cooperate with the consortium. His opponent was subjected to careful interviews, while Helms offered provocative sound bites, which the press was compelled to report. While the coverage was more reasonable, with more information about the candidates' positions on pressing problems, the campaign was primarily conducted through political advertising, which was no more elevated than it had been in the past.

Less ambitious moves in the direction of public journalism were discernable throughout the country. *The Virginia-Pilot* organized "community conversations" to discern the views of the citizens and inform how it would cover community issues. *The Spokesman-Review* of Spokane, Washington, abandoned the use of tradition editorials and instead had two "interactive editors" who assisted readers in writing their own opinion pieces. The *San Jose Mercury News* ran letters from readers throughout the paper, shaping the reporting and the form of the news.[12] And on an integrated national stage, local citizens forums were conducted throughout the country during the national election campaign of 1996, which led to a special national convention where the citizenry discussed the problems of the day. The gathering received extensive coverage and portions were broadcast nationwide by public radio and public television stations.

Each of these experiments in public journalism represented an attempt to overcome the limitations of prevailing journalistic practices. Note that these moves were not partisan; rather they involved a concern for professional ethics and responsibilities. Journalists, committed to their profession, perceived a problem in the rules of the game. Although they did not want to be partisan, they perceived that the stance of objectively reporting the news undermined their capacity to fulfill their responsibility to inform their readers as citizens. They discussed among themselves strategies to address this dilemma.

Criticisms of public journalism came from both the left and the right and resembled criticisms of public opinion polling. Journalists were criticized for taking too much responsibility and for taking too little. One thing, however, was indisputable: the alternative conventions of public journalism were indeed different from the prevailing practices in most of the media.

It was the focus of public journalism on the quality of public life that opened it to this broad range of criticisms. In North Carolina and the other cases I have mentioned, these new journalistic practices promoted the inclusion of the public in three distinct ways: (1) as a constructed fictive body, depicted by polls, which determined what issues were to be addressed and how (that polls were thus central to the new journalism was controversial), (2) as a group of individuals who discuss the issues of the day and need to be assisted by journalists, who at times went out to the political periphery to find out what people were discussing and to help them discuss it more broadly and effectively, and (3) as a group of political actors needing to address political issues (thus some involved in the public journalism movement have attempted to organize their communities to address issues like poor government services in depressed neighborhoods, crime, education, and so forth). I have emphasized the first two types of practices, because it seems to me that these were what was really most original about the movement and most important in shaping American public life. The third approach to the public of public journalism was a political and a public-relations temptation—it was attractive for a local newspaper to be able to claim responsibility for clean and safe streets in its community. But such activity was clearly political and left media very much open to the criticism that it was substituting political activity for journalism.

Focusing on this dimension of the public journalism movement, veteran *New York Times* editor and writer Max Frankel dismissed it as little more than fix-it journalism, a kind of upper-class community-service approach to the news.[13] But Frankel, along with other mainstream critics, did not take seriously the public journalism movement's concern for the care of the public space, which was at the core of its project, as it related to both the public of public opinion polls and the discursive public. Nonetheless, it was this concern with the possible politicization of the news that was the greatest weakness of the public journalism movement. It was most vulnerable to the charge that journalists in the movement were not only reporting the news but attempting to make it.

The debate about public journalism has not been conclusive. As a distinct group of journalists advocating a new approach to journalism, it has faded. It affected local reporting to some degree, as well as political reporting in the mid-1990s. But its lasting effects can be found in less explicit form. It opened a debate about journalistic responsibility for polit-

ical reporting that has been incorporated into more conventional journalistic practices. The way the *New York Times* has developed and covered the issue of race is a case in point, as is the way it has dealt with the
trauma of September 11, 2001.[14] Frankel may have been one of the leading critics of public journalism, but one can discern how the innovations
of public journalism have affected the way the paper of record reports the
news. In the series "How Race Is Lived in America," the *Times* went well
beyond the headlines and newsworthy events to do fifteen reports on race
as an enduring underlying dimension of American life. A large number
of reporters went out and listened to how people across the nation
thought and talked about race, and this formed the basis of their reports.
The series sought to inform our understanding of race. It certainly was fit
to print, as the *Times*'s slogan puts it, but it was not in a standard sense
news. Similarly, the "Portraits in Grief" series published after 9/11 followed the tenets of public journalism more closely than traditional notions of journalistic responsibility. The form of the reports, brief portraits
of the victims of the attacks of September 11, was modeled on the signs
and descriptions posted all over New York by relatives desperately seeking information about the missing, and nurtured an understanding of the
human dimension of the tragedy, outside of political position and nationalist assertion.

Thus elements of public journalism are now built into conventional
institutional practices. The reform indicates that news, as a cultural form,
develops not simply by serving the powers or their opposition, but as an
independent institution. Journalism as a profession had, in the early
1990s, judged its coverage of presidential politics to be inadequate, and
a group of journalists had formulated an alternative and created space
for experimentation. As an alternative ethical system and guideline for
practice, the proposal was considered by others and rejected, but it has
nonetheless affected the way the news is presented. Again we see that
small things matter.

Democracy Is in the Details

Education and journalism both discipline, both prepare people to serve
the existing order. Schools, from kindergartens to universities, prepare
students to serve the powers, and they place students into positions that
reflect the existing injustices of the social order. Similarly, journalists at
major newspapers and magazines make it appear that the existing historical order is the natural order. They may be critical at the edges, but
overwhelmingly are supportive of the status quo. There were important

differences between the *New York Times* and *Pravda* in the cold war era, but they were alike in that they supported the social order, portraying the dominant rules of the game as both inevitable and just.

These gross generalizations are not, to my mind, even half truths. What is most important about a free, liberal education is that it does have a critical component, even as it prepares the young for vocational positions in the established social hierarchy. What is most important about the comparison between the *Times* and *Pravda* is that the definition of the news was a problematic matter in the former and was administered by a political elite in the latter. The real promise and meaning of free institutions of higher learning and journalism is in the details: what goes on between and among students and teachers, journalists and readers. The examples of one college seminar and of a reform movement in journalism have indicated how the field of the politics of small things is constituted within established cultural institutions, and with consequential results.

In the churches of the religious right, the truth and politics became too intimately associated. It has become common for those involved with this movement to denounce the bias of the liberal elite. Those on the left in turn often denounce cultural institutions as instruments of global capital and American hegemony. But it is not the political coloration of institutions that is most significant. It is rather that they establish a field for free public interaction, which exists, or does not, in the details of the social interactions. This is an accomplishment of the politics of small things.

The stakes are much higher, more visible, and have broader impact when television illuminates small things, a phenomenon to which we now turn. We will consider another small site suggested by our analysis thus far but not examined explicitly. It is less the consequence of intentional projects of political action than the result of the presentation of self in televisual life. Our examination of the media thus far has been informed by a consideration of the work of Arendt and Goffman, with an emphasis on Arendt. We have focused on intentional strategic action through the new and old media. Before we conclude, I will change the emphasis a little, emphasizing Goffman's sensibility, turning to the expressive dimension.

8

The Presentation of Self in the Age of Electronic Communications

Television did not play a significant role in the political struggles in the old Soviet bloc. The revolutions of 1989 were televised only in their last stages, and the televisual presentation was little more than a dramatic postscript.[1] To be sure, the violent battle between those loyal to the old order and those loyal to the transition authorities in Romania took place outside the central television studios, but this was a battle over an instrument. It was not a politics constituted through the media.

This contrasts strikingly with the wars of the terrorists and antiterrorists, and with the situation of normal democratic politics in our times. The decisive definition of the situation now appears on television, a distinctive and increasingly central media form. If a situation is defined as real, or appears and is perceived as real, on television, it becomes real in its consequences.

The Dean campaign was clearly over, not when he lost the Iowa caucus vote, but when he followed up with his "I had a scream" speech. He appeared unbalanced, out of control, lacking judgment. He tried afterward to change that appearance, to redefine himself during a number of television appearances, but it did not work. His appearance fit a perception about him, and the perception stuck.

This televisual power of definition is not superficial or

silly, although it is often presented as such. It is in fact an important dimension of power: something that democrats and antidemocrats, terrorists and antiterrorists keep in mind.

Osama bin Laden understood when he was interviewed in 1996 that the platform for terrorism is the media, specifically television.[2] The attacks of September 11, 2001, were produced for and experienced through television. They were seen and experienced in real time throughout the world, and this was meant to be the case. Those who created the spectacle judged their success by the response to televised images, and those who were attacked perceived the attack in the same way. What made the event of central importance was not the loss of life. Nor was the power of the United States militarily challenged. There was, though, the experience of vulnerability, which was televised and observed globally.

This is true of terrorism more generally. Suicide bombings have spread from the occupied territories of Palestine to civilian aircraft flying the American skies to occupied Iraq. Each of these locations is both central and peripheral. While the actual act does occur in a specific place at a specific time, the time and place are also the stage set for further-reaching political communication. There were the immediate experiences in lower Manhattan and in Washington to the suicide attacks of 2001. There have been similar experiences, each manifested in a specific time and place, in Israel, Palestine, and Iraq. But the political consequences of the attacks have been dependent mostly on their appearance on television, first in real time and then as the images are repeated through time. The televised images of these acts become the political reality. Arendt argues that in politics appearances are realities.[3] In the televisual age, the appearances are televised.

Acts of terror and of war are not small. The Dean scream and the like are. And such small things, small gestures, presentations of self, can and have played a significant role in history. Television can transform the smallest gestures into very big things. The medium has an expressive dimension. It is something that makes small things especially important in our dark times.

It has often been noted that John F. Kennedy won the presidential debates with Richard Nixon in 1960 because he appeared more appealing on television. This has been taken to indicate the superficiality of American politics. There is a nostalgia for debates of the past, for the Lincoln-Douglas debates. Back in 1858, Abraham Lincoln and Stephen Douglas confronted each other substantially, addressing serious matters, the pressing issue of slavery as the nation stood at the brink of a civil war. A century later, Kennedy defeated Nixon because of his glamour. If this were the case, ours would indeed be a sorry state. This sad situation has been noted repeatedly in popular commentaries and in scholarly tomes.[4] Yet, as Michael Schudson has shown in a brilliant analysis of American public life, the nineteenth-century debate was as much about entertainment as was the twentieth-century one.[5] The fact that Nixon was deemed the winner by those who listened to the debate on radio, while Kennedy won according to those who watched it on television, does not indicate anything about the quality of the confrontation. It simply reveals that Nixon was more expressively adept at radio presentation, Kennedy at television presentation. And it should be added, as Schudson does, that the favorable judgment of the Lincoln-Douglas debates reflects a preference for the nineteenth-century style of oration, and particularly for Lincoln's literary eloquence.

Expressive eloquence is important, and this is appreciated in the case of the literary.[6] It is generally recognized that Lincoln was one of the great presidents, if not the greatest, in the history of the United States. He led the nation through its greatest trauma. Arguably the Civil War, or "the war between the states" as partisans of and those nostalgic for the Confederacy call it, was about much more than either expression suggests. It was a second American Revolution, formulated through Lincoln's words.[7] His greatness is directly attached to his eloquence. He redefined American political culture.

This was an expressive literary feat, most dramatically rendered in the Gettysburg Address.[8] Lincoln presented a reinterpretation of the national story, turning the Declaration of Independence and the notion of equality into the central proposition of the national culture: "Four score and seven years ago our fathers brought forth on this continent a new nation, conceived in liberty and dedicated to the proposition that all men are created equal." With dense meaning, and concrete and clear expression, Lincoln guided a nation through tragedy and suffering toward a new project that is still very real and still incomplete. The power of the word and its connection to political leadership was never more clearly evident. Lincoln was one of America's great writers and, as such, one of its great leaders. His words, written and spoken, persuaded.

Persuasion is differently realized in our changed media landscape. Oddly, the grammatical correctness of John Kerry's speech provoked much negative commentary during the course of the 2004 presidential campaign.[9] The fact that as the Democratic candidate he spoke clearly and in a formally correct manner indicated that he was out of touch with ordinary people. Such accomplishment, it was said, seems to the American citizenry to express haughtiness, to reveal the speaker's distance from his democratic audience. This audience is, though, persuaded by electronic eloquence.[10]

It may be that the audience watching Kennedy in his debate with Nixon was persuaded by the strength and warmth of Kennedy's personality when he appeared on television. But it is just as likely that the radio audience was persuaded by Nixon, by the assurance and manliness that he expressed through his style of oral presentation. Schudson, a young man in the Midwest in 1960, recalled listening to the debate and thinking that Kennedy sounded prissy.[11] His Boston accent sounded a bit effeminate, not quite American, perhaps of the British upper class. The contrast between the support Kennedy received from those who watched the debate on television and the support Nixon received from those who listened on radio underscores, not the superficiality of judgment in the age of television, but different forms of expressive eloquence and persuasion.

The small matter of presentation through the written word made it possible for Lincoln to lead. Now the issue revolves around television expression. That Americans did not overwhelmingly choose Al Gore over George Bush may very well have turned on an apparently trivial matter. Gore appeared as a patronizing bore on television. He switched between hot and cold expression in the presidential debates. His televisual presentation of self was unappealing, and enough of the electorate chose not to have him in their homes that he lost the election.

Many made their decision because they did not like the way Gore acted on TV. Simple people voted for a candidate who had little national experience over one who had a great deal of experience and who had supported the policies of a popular standing president. This does seem silly. But if we keep in mind the importance of eloquence in political leadership, the decision is not trivial at all, even if one judges it as mistaken. A key to political power is the ability to persuade citizens to act in common cause, to lead them. If a president is wooden when he speaks to the citizenry on television, if he does not have *the power of televisual presentation of self*, he lacks a significant resource for political mobilization and is less likely to be an effective leader. Expression is a key component of social interaction, as the work of Goffman reveals, and a deficit in expressive capacity makes effective leadership less possible.

This small dimension of politics also opens and closes the capacity for freedom. It was necessary in the Polish literary salon for the participants to work together to make the event appear as a literary event, not an illegal gathering in a private apartment. It was also necessary for the participants in my liberal arts seminar to define their gathering as a real learning situation and not simply a place for schooling. As such small things are expressed through television, the quality of expression becomes very important to the sustaining of freedom and political creativity. As we have seen, this was quite evidently the problem with Howard Dean.

Constituting Public Space through the Mediated Presentation of Self

The Dean campaign lost its power, at least in part, due to the expressive failures of its leader on television. It may also be that his substantive positions on the electoral issues were less popular than those of his rivals or that voters judged him to be insufficiently prepared for high office. Yet, since other candidates had as little preparation and since the positions of all the Democratic primary candidates were fairly similar, his defeat probably had more to do with his presentation of self on television. Partisans account for this by referring to a media conspiracy, and indeed the logic of the mainstream media did make the going tough for the Dean campaign. Once he was declared the frontrunner, even before the primaries were held, he was subjected to very close media scrutiny, some of it clearly ill willed (particularly on the Fox network, as discussed in chapter 5). His rivals encouraged this. They attacked him relentlessly when it seemed that he would be the Democratic nominee. The party establishment was clearly uncomfortable with the Dean candidacy, as Dean's supporters clearly understood, and the establishment thus encouraged the anti-Dean pileup. Dean did not handle this well. He spent money recklessly. He attacked when he should have been conciliatory, and he was conciliatory when he should have attacked. The overall impression he gave was not very attractive, and the scream did him in.

Nevertheless, something special was created by the Dean campaign, with potentially lasting importance. The challenge for Dean supporters and for those interested in sustaining alternative democratic political action is to notice what was accomplished and to act accordingly. They need to appreciate the public space constituted by their interactions. The Dean campaign gave those committed to an antiwar position a capacity to go beyond the "no" that had been the linguistic limit of the movement. But as the contrast between the democratic position in Poland and Czechoslovakia (discussed in chapter 3) suggested, this richer power of definition is fully developed through time and in a complex social space. This is something that both Dean and the chief architect of his Internet strategy, Joe Trippi, worked on.

Trippi began addressing this challenge even before the campaign was over. In a last-ditch effort to save his candidacy, Dean appointed a more conventional campaign chief, Roy Neel. Trippi understood this for what

it was, a demotion. He resigned from the campaign, while still expressing strong support for the candidate and for all those who were still working for him. It was at this point that the difference between the Dean campaign and an ordinary campaign for elective office became apparent.
There were no explicit recriminations. Dean at the end seemed to hope
that a campaign chief of a more traditional variety might put him into
contention in the Wisconsin primary, and that this might save his candidacy. Trippi continued to support Dean but realized that they had come
up short and started thinking about the state of the movement after the
candidacy. Dean soon would follow the same path.

Dean and Trippi shared an understanding that the task at hand was
to somehow institutionalize the social movement and its virtual interactive base, to make the force generated by this individual candidacy into
an ongoing presence in the Democratic Party. This would require mar-
shalling the participants of the Dean movement, first, to support the
Democratic nominee for president in 2004 and, second, to support who
they considered to be progressive candidates in state and local elections.
Dean and Trippi also encouraged movement activists to seek public office. There was an understanding that a new form of mobilization and
fund-raising had been created and that it had to be applied to the practical task of reforming the Democratic Party. This was the way to transform
American politics.

But there was a problem. On Trippi's new blog, Change for America,
and Dean's, Blog for America, there was a great deal of resistance to their
strategy. Many supported it but were not sure how to proceed, while others found the move to a third-party or independent candidate, such as
Ralph Nader, more appealing. Still others seemed to have had their previously existing cynicism reaffirmed by the fate of the Dean candidacy.
The establishment was not going to permit such an independent political
force to prevail; the nature of its power was again revealed by its thwart-
ing Dean. Such "Deaniacs" came to think that they should not have been
so naïve as to think that they could make a difference.

Trippi's expressive skills, his Internet eloquence, had made a significant contribution to gathering support for Dean's candidacy. Those
skills, and their capacity to counter cynicism, were again demonstrated
at the moment of the primary defeat, as the movement was being recali-
brated. The campaign still had a few weeks ahead of it, but Trippi was on
the sidelines, thinking about the future. He introduced his blog using an
unassuming voice, asking others to join him in what he hoped would be
the continuation of a mass movement:[12]

This is where I intend to keep, in my own small way, my part in the changing of America and our politics going. I am hoping that others who have ideas and energy to continue building a different kind of politics based on people, grassroots and netroots will exchange them here, and make a difference together in 2004 and beyond.

I am still trying to figure out what I am actually going to do with the rest of my life, so far it's always been about changing or messing with something bigger than me.

The one thing I know I want to do, is continue to do my part to build a community with a mission of changing our country for the better.

So here starts a new blog.

I am proud of what so many in the Dean campaign accomplished these past 13 or so months. Governor Dean and the grassroots campaign that rallied to the cause gave the Democratic Party back its voice. Standing up to George Bush when most feared his popularity. Opposing the war in Iraq when others were silent. Building an energized grassroots while others laughed. Proving that the hundreds of thousands of small donors could raise more than those addicted to big money politics.

Regardless of the outcome in the Democratic nomination fight—thousands of Americans came together to show a new and different way, and a new and different medium (the Internet) has emerged as a force and tool for the people to reclaim their voice in the party and in our democracy.

The future of politics in our country has already been changed because of the work and dedication of people working together to make a difference.

No one is going to change America for you. You have to work for the change you want—and you have to get other Americans to join your cause.

Change for America is my attempt to continue to do just that—so join in, comment away, and let's continue the fight to rid our country of the Bush administration (the first step to real change).

I don't have much in tech support as of yet, but over time I hope this blog will be a lot better than it is today—kind of reminds me of those days 13 months or so ago—when there were only a few of us and we started the ugliest blog in America—the

Call to Action blog. It helped to launch something special, hope-
fully the Change for America Blog humble as it is will launch
something special as well.

Thank you for reading and participating.

The Next American Revolution is only just beginning.

There were two hundred responses to this initial posting, and they too
had a clearly personal tone. Trippi was revealing himself as a vulnerable
person, committed to change but unsure of what to do at this point. He
opened space for reflection on alternatives and for personal revelations.
His readers responded in kind. They shared with each other an appreciation of what he had done, and he in turn posted more messages paying
tribute to them. At this point, they were just talking to each other.

But there was a trajectory. Participants started by sharing their feelings and reflections on their experiences, but then they moved on to a discussion about how to proceed further. They debated how to intervene in
the elections. They discussed alternative Web designs. They considered
whether the efforts of those most committed to Trippi should be parallel
to, or coordinated with, the work of Dean and his group. Alternative
strategic paths were suggested. But in the first weeks after the defeat of
their preferred candidate, the commentators were most strikingly engaged
in face work, as Goffman would put it. They were working to maintain
each other's dignity and to define their situation as one in which they
could still work together on social change.

In the following comment, observe both the face work and the important strategic suggestion:

> The problem is that a lot of people are taking away the message
> that none of this worked if we are/were unable to get Howard
> into office. They're turning off their passion and turning on their
> apathy.
>
> We need a way to convince them that we've already won a
> previously unthinkable victory, and I'm afraid our words just
> won't be enough for many.
>
> I think maybe we need not just an organization to come out
> of this, but also an incredible, highly-visible project, right out of
> the gate. Something we can accomplish so that people will sit
> back up and say, "Hey, wait a minute! These people are still there,
> and they're still making a real difference!"
>
> I wonder if there's some way to set up a way to track our do-
> nations to Congressional races. A multiple "bat" page, of sorts,

but with donations that go directly to the candidate's coffers (since I presume there'd be FEC issues with having donations go through "us" centrally first).

In the purely navel-gazing, selfish category, I'd love to see a Sleepless Spring tour to thank the grassroots for all our work. Ah well. I can dream. :-)

I'm serious about a major, attention-grabbing project, though. We need to wake up not just the media, but our own disillusioned supporters as well. (Posted by cdmarine, February 16, 2004)

"Cdmarine" is pointing to a challenge that many in the movement were well aware of, the need to make the emerging movement visible to the outside world. In debating Dean's television performances, a concern shared by many on the left was expressed, concerning the need for some alternative to the major media to reach a broad audience. This is where the right's use of talk radio is much envied. The expressive work after the defeat was within the movement, but the need for expressive work outside the movement was recognized, as well as uncertainty about how to proceed. The first larger audience would have to be the Democratic Party. The broader public would follow.

To be sure, the message of these activists had already become broadly visible to some extent. As Dean's focus was assimilated by all the Democratic presidential candidates and particularly by John Kerry, the winner of the primaries, and by the Democratic Party in general, the message was being institutionalized. Democrats were directly challenging Republicans on principle. Alternative ways of financing elections had been revealed. The nature of political discourse had been transformed, as we observed in chapter 5. But there was the additional challenge of maintaining the free public space that had been created. This is what the participants in Trippi's Change for America and Dean's Blog for America were trying to accomplish in their interactions with each other.

The "Lost Treasure of the Revolutionary Tradition" and Internet Activism

The special character of the power that the Dean supporters constituted in their interactions may easily be overlooked, since it does not fit into established ways of thinking about politics either in popular or more informed theoretical discussions. It is not just that Dean and his supporters developed a way to raise a lot of money, or that they discovered a new way for an outsider to challenge the party regulars. Rather, the Dean campaign revealed once again the possibilities of citizens bringing something radically new into the world, a way of doing politics freely in the age of terrorism and antiterrorism.

We have observed throughout this inquiry the capacity people have to bring something new into the world, in historic situations but also in everyday interactions. This capacity Arendt called "the lost treasure of the revolutionary tradition." She appreciated particularly how this treasure was manifested in the American Revolution and how it fleetingly appeared at times of radical transformation throughout the modern era: during the French Revolution, among the committees but not the Jacobins, during the Russian Revolution, among the Soviets but not the Bolsheviks, in the French resistance to the Nazi occupation in the 1940s, and among the workers councils during the Hungarian Revolt of 1956. She recalled how Thomas Jefferson wanted to build into the new republic a system of councils, which would facilitate the institutionalization of this capacity, which she recognized as public freedom. She believed that of all the modern revolutions, it was the American Revolution in which public freedom was most central. And she thought that this treasure of revolutionary activity had been neglected by political theory and thereby lost.

This tradition of freedom has been lost, though, not only because of the relative neglect of the importance of the American Revolution or because free public action as an end in itself is not appreciated. It also has been lost because its roots in the everyday power of social definition have not been appreciated, even by Arendt. And most practically, it has been lost because of the failure to institutionalize the free open activity so as to provide it with a regular system of social support. For the work to be institutionalized, it must first be perceived. Then the work of supporting it can occur. It must be understood as being important. In terms of this inquiry, it is necessary to come to understand the importance of the politics of small things.

The antiwar movement mobilized citizens globally, but the war proceeded. The Dean campaign developed a capacity to raise huge sums of money from hundreds of thousands of people of modest means, but ultimately the candidate did not prevail in the Democratic primaries. Dean's project was extended to the Kerry campaign, which again ended in defeat, overwhelmed by the micropolitics of the religious right. The failure to achieve the most explicit results makes it seem that these movements did not amount to much. There was the end, preventing a foolish unilateral war and this failed, both as part of the antiwar movement and as championed by the Dean and Kerry campaigns. This leads some to despair, not appreciating that their actions had significance as ends in themselves.

That such actions can be ends in themselves was most evident during the communist period in the democratic opposition. In fact, in that case, the participants had little reason to believe that they would ever during their lifetimes bring into being a transformed political order with formal freedoms. They understood, though, that if they were able to sustain their independent activity, they would be successful. They easily settled upon constituting their freedoms by acting freely.

The situation in liberal democracies in the age of terror and antiterror, in a globalized landscape, reveals that formal freedom is not enough, but this does not mean that constituted alternatives are less important. Quite the contrary, here and now, the need to provide consequential alternatives to dominant modes of understanding and action is pressing. With nuclear arms proliferating and terrorism becoming a commonplace, and with the global superpower confronting these developments in an arrogant fashion that is understood by many as undermining the capacity to avoid terror and fundamentalism, the need for the politics of small things is very great. It is very important to realize that it is the means of opposing, more than the short-term realization of the ends, that is most crucial. It is necessary for the superpower to understand that there are practical means to prevent terrorism that are both less threatening and more likely to be successful. It is necessary for potential terrorists to realize that there are alternatives to terror, more likely to achieve their ends.

I know that this may sound blithely idealistic. But let me be clear. I am not suggesting that engaging in small group action is the way to fight terrorism directly or that it is the alternative to globalization and American hegemony. I am maintaining, rather, that it is in the interaction among people, and in their capacity to redefine their situation and to act in concert, that alternatives to terrorism and antiterrorism and religious fundamentalism will be realized. Other actions may be necessary, perhaps even sometimes war, but wars against the hyperpower and against terrorism cannot be won without the politics of small things.

Even on the democratic stage, as the antiwar activists and Dean supporters consider their activities, they should understand that the power they have constituted is something that could last or could disappear depending on their actions. It is the form of the constitution of their power that is central, not the achievement of their particular ends, the election Howard Dean and averting or ending a war that they deem to be unjust.

I think that it is very important to recognize the formal creativity and broad formal significance of the Internet activism of the antiwar movement and the Dean campaign. In their activities the online activists created something new, the possibility of a true political life. As Arendt puts it: "The actual content of political life [is] . . . the joy and gratification that arise out of being in company with our peers, out of acting together and appearing in public, out of inserting ourselves into the world by word and deed, thus acquiring and sustaining our personal identity and beginning something entirely new."[13] They in fact helped create a more vibrant polis. Again quoting Arendt: "The polis, properly speaking, is not the city state in its physical location; it is the organization of the people as it arises out of acting and speaking together, and its true space lies between people living together for this purpose, no matter where they happen to be."[14] A new form of engaging in a creative politics was created. This, more than any other factor, given the politics of fear and desperation that exists in our world, is of greatest importance.

I do not mean to say that this new domain of politics is without specific normative content. Indeed, it has had a specific political complexion, and this is very significant. The Internet form of the politics of small things has made it possible for the left to make sense, in a way that it had not for decades. The politics of small things through the Internet may well be the left's answer to right-wing talk radio. We will explore this as we conclude our inquiry. But before turning to this substantive normative issue, a few more words about the expressive dimension in the age of electronic media are in order.

The Expressive Dimension and Politics: Face-to-Face Interaction, Television, and the Internet

The expressive dimension was central to Goffman's dramaturgical sociology. He showed how people come to create their social reality through their expressive interactions. He did not systematically explore the political dimensions of the reality they constitute, but these are clearly present, as we have observed. If people can present themselves in everyday life and, in concert, create their social reality, there is power in their actions, the very power that Arendt describes as being distinctively political as opposed to coercive. In each of the snapshots from the Polish democratic underground described in chapter 1, we saw how this was related to a central political struggle in our recent past. When people act as if they live in a free society, when they express to each other the conviction that they are free and together create the bonds of a free social order, they will, if their actions persist, create freedom. In this inquiry, I have highlighted how this works in relation to the central political questions of our political times, but also how it works away from the central political stage, in a university seminar and in professional association.

While television extends the reach of the power of social definition and confuses traditional distinctions between public and private, the same expressive dynamics are present. The way public figures appear on television, the way they express themselves and the way they are depicted, defines political reality. This often leads to a spectacular conflict, carefully staged and managed, as was most evident in the case of the impeachment of President Clinton.

Clinton was a televisually brilliant politician. He, like his gifted predecessor and counterpart on the right, Ronald Reagan, could express a warmth and intimacy directly to television viewers. They appeared credible when they claimed they felt their constituent's pain and seemed to have a direct personal relationship with the public. Clinton perfected the town meeting format. He would listen carefully to his questioners, seemingly focusing all attention on them, and then he would speak to the camera as if it was an individual person, while actually he was speaking to millions. In such a context, he answered serious questions of state, but also the infamous question about whether he wore boxers or briefs.

He and Reagan understood that public rhetoric had become intimate,[15] but Clinton was ultimately done in by this. His impeachment was about making his private life a matter of public concern. He was not the first president to have an extramarital affair. He was not even the first president to engage in such affairs recklessly. But in that his activities became public, were on television, he had to address them on television. The battle between Clinton and special prosecutor Ken Starr was televised, from appearances on the television magazine *Sixty Minutes* to live coverage of the impeachment hearings. In retrospect, we can see that the threat of terrorism was mounting, unseen on television, while the nation was preoccupied with such urgent issues as the definition of the words *sex* and *is*.[16] What was on television seemed real. What was not became real only later, when it was televised.

Expression plays a less spectacular, more interactive role on the Internet than on television, something more like its role in face-to-face communication. How bloggers appear to each other sustains or cuts off interaction. The way they express themselves, the way they come to feel that they have a personal connection, is a key to constituting a virtual political reality. As we have seen, Dean did not just use the Internet as an instrument, as a machine that could be turned on and off. A virtual polis was created through expressive interactions, in many ways creating Dean as a candidate, and this was something that he recognized.

Trippi knew that he could not simply redirect Dean's Internet supporters to new political purposes when the campaign ended. They had to continue their interaction and together develop a capacity to act in new directions. For this form of expressive politics to work, the participants had to maintain their active involvement. The Internet-mediated politics of small things is more like a seminar room than like a political advertisement on television or a broadcast sound byte. It is mutually sustaining and interactive. The involvement of the participants is relatively equally distributed. It is much more egalitarian, much less hierarchical, more deliberative. This has clear political implications.

Conclusion: The Politics of the Politics of Small Things

We started with glimpses of the politics around kitchen tables, in an underground bookstore, and at an illegal poetry reading. We moved on to Polish theater performances in 1968 and the streets of Bucharest, Prague, and Warsaw in 1989. We then considered the networks of terror that supported the attacks of September 11, 2001, and the official and unofficial responses to the attacks. As Vaclav Havel's fictive personifications of the politics of small things, his greengrocer and brewer, illuminated our analysis of the last century, the two lovers in Arundhati Roy's novel *The God of Small Things* suggested a way to perceive the sociological texture of democratic alternatives to terror and antiterrorism now. We then analyzed the virtual politics of small things in the antiwar movement and Howard Dean's presidential campaign and the micropolitics of the Christian right, critically distinguishing the power and normative qualities of the politics of small things. This led us to a consideration of how small things work within established institutional practices: in a liberal arts seminar and among professional journalists. While recognizing that large things, the power of the communist and anticommunist states and the power of terrorists and state antiterrorists, have certainly been politically significant, we observed how the small ones have been as significant. They are overlooked with very dangerous consequences: some, thinking that there are no alternatives, embrace terrorism, and others, a self-defeating antiterrorism.

The power of the politics of small things was described, and, crucially, its potential as a normative alternative to the politics of discipline and coercion was highlighted. It is not that all small-scale political activity provides a normative alternative. The normative alternative appears when a space is opened in human interaction for a freedom that creates power. This was observable in the opposition to the powers in the old Soviet bloc, and it has been again visible in the antiwar movement and the Dean campaign and in daily practices of education and journalism. Our sites of critical investigation have been human interactions, both embodied and virtual, where changes in the definition of a situation have created the possibility of large-scale consequences.

This space for freedom need not have a particular political content. Those in the political opposition in Poland included secularists and Catholics, political liberals, conservatives, and socialists. Yet there sometimes is a link between the form of the politics of small things and particular political content. In that the democratic movement in Poland was almost exclusively based in the politics of small things, the form of the activity did have specific political consequences. The rules of the political game shaped its political message. The opposition was the very opposite of totalitarianism. Given this context, it was democratic both in form and in content.

Lech Walesa and other union activists often maintained that Solidarność, the independent trade union, was explicitly not a political organization. They were just defending their rights as workers, rights guaranteed in the socialist constitution. The unionists recognized "the leading role of the Communist Party," as loyalty to the system was officially rendered. They accepted the communist system as inevitable, given geopolitical realities. They just wanted to carve out a space for their own independent activities, defending worker rights. Yet observers in Poland and abroad took this to be an affectation, a pretense. Clearly an independent union in a totalitarian order was a challenge. It was political. Even a declaration that one is apolitical is a form of politics in an overpoliticized world.

Both the appearance of the apolitical and the underlying reality of the political had a truth to them. Solidarity was not formed to be an opposition political force; its politics of small things did not have a particular content. Yet the independent space it created was an oppositional force. In a polity based upon official edicts and truths, there was a space for people to meet, talk, and act upon their common concerns. This is political power, as Arendt understood it, but it is not just any sort of political power. It has democratic content, which was evident in Poland as it turned away from demagogic temptations after the fall of the old regime.

The same pattern can be observed in American politics today. Of course, the context for the politics of small things is not totalitarian. Free debate is found across the political spectrum. Yet consequential dogma is found primarily on one side of the political spectrum, and, therefore the politics of small things favors those on the other side. Discursive politics is favored by the politics of small things. Assertive demagogic politics is not—and this too has specific political content. The virtual politics of small things on the Internet, we have observed, stands as a progressive alternative to the politics of the dogmatic right. This is not an accident.

The Dogmatic Right and Talk Radio

Since the time of the Reagan revolution—really since the time of the Vietnam war, or at least since the end of the movement that opposed it—the political right has been ascendant in the United States, while the left has been on the run. The right has made sense to the general public, while the left has not.[1] A combination of factors contributed to this situation. The perceived failures of the welfare state, or at least its limitations in achieving its stated goals, and the absolute failure of socialism as a systemic alternative to capitalism, put state intervention into question. This questioning of statism was persuasive because it was not consistent. While it celebrated the successes of the free market, it actually did not attack social welfare for the middle class, prominently social security. The appeal of simple policies of tax cuts, combined with bold patriotic rhetoric, simple moral declaration, and a touch of xenophobia and racism of a relatively subtle sort ("equal rights for whites"), added to the right-wing advantage. The left was put on the defensive. The weakening of the left intensified with the fall of Soviet socialism. Those who maintained that this was a victory for capitalism presented a position that was readily understood.

Further, a new form of media appeal supported the rightist common sense in a decidedly dogmatic fashion. Here the elastic figure of Ronald Reagan was central. His personal charisma, articulated with the refined televisual expressive skills of a professional actor, opened up opportunities for a complex political coalition. Reagan presented himself as the tough guy, the steadfast patriot willing to take on the "evil empire," and as the congenial nice guy, the "Gipper," who smiled warmly and empathized, felt the pain of others, was willing to sacrifice, and acted. There were conflicting ideological currents that contributed to the "Reagan revolution."

Reagan had the support of the neoconservatives, mostly concerned with the anticommunist struggle and with the limits of the welfare state, and the support of the moral majoritarians, the Christian right, motivated by a cultural war against secular humanism.

There were obviously great tensions between these supporters, the Christian right and those who were most deeply committed to the anti-statist pursuit of a purely realized free market. At the time, Reagan's presentation of self kept them at peace. There was no need to develop a unified ideological manifesto that rationally synthesized these competing demands of the ascendant right's various elements. The televised charisma of Ronald Reagan seemed to do the trick.

But actually more was involved. There were significant media supports for this charisma.[2] One was the targeted mailing list. The other was the increasingly popular form of talk radio, a dogmatic media form.

Targeted mailings were relatively simple. Highly motivated individuals with distinctive political concerns—those who opposed abortion or gun control, those who supported prayer in schools, the death penalty, or tax cuts—were identified and sent appeals to fund and vote for the president and the Republican Party as a way of addressing those concerns. Each appeal and the resulting activism occurred independently. If interest groups happened to overlap that was fine, but they could as easily have opposing concerns. This was segmented political action, a coalition facilitated by the symbol of the charismatic leader.

Talk radio, on the other hand, has been more synthetic and more combative, with sustained importance.[3] While there were no manifestos uniting the right, the dogmatic assertiveness of talk radio figures, most prominently Rush Limbaugh, did present a synthetic partisan approach. The synthesis has been based less on reason than on dramatic assertion: All those who differ from the right-wing talk show host are fools. Day after day, the limitations of the media liberals, the environmentalists, the abortionists, the left-wingers, the godless, and so on are condemned in no uncertain terms. Anger, certainty, and humor are mixed freely. It is really all a show, but it has very serious consequences. It galvanizes the like-minded, leaves them ready to be called into action. It presents a dogmatic common sense to an identifiable community of listeners. It mobilizes the community through periodic calls to action, most spectacularly in the anti-Clinton zealotry that resulted in the drive to impeachment. The talk radio form is a sort of broad narrowcasting. The audience is large but not all are invited, only the true believers, though others may listen in for the entertainment value.

The popularity of the political talk radio form has presented a puzzle to those on the left. It is a form monopolized by the right. While the population is evenly divided between left and right, attempts to create liberal talk radio have repeatedly failed. This is partially a result of a kind of self-fulfilling prophecy. There is an expectation that talk radio is a right-wing phenomenon, so only those interested in rightist entertainment tune in. When leftists attempt to present an alternative, they do not deliver what the audience is looking for. If this is an adequate explanation of the situation, there may be good cause for liberals to try again, and very visibly, to let it be known broadly that a liberal talk radio is being produced and to create an audience. This is the approach of Air America Radio.[4]

But if we consider the problem as part of a broader historical movement, the limits of this approach become apparent. Talk radio as a cultural form of dogmatic and entertaining assertiveness works for an audience of right-wing true believers. The embattled position of the left makes such a form less salient on the left. At a time when certainty on the left is not common, the authoritarian voice is not persuasive. The left wants and needs popular debate. This also suggests that the leftist Internet, with its significant deliberative capacities, may be the real alternative to right-wing talk radio.

Democratic Discourse, the Left, and the Internet

There is a sense in which Bill Clinton was the liberal answer to Ronald Reagan. Like Reagan, he rallied the support of diverse segments of his party. They included Democrats pushing a more conservative social approach, including a critique of "welfare as we know it," as well as traditionalists, people concerned with maintaining the social "safety net," free traders, along with trade unionists, social conservatives and social liberals, people on both sides of the cultural wars. Clinton's expressive performance attracted the support of a broad range of supporters. Yet he did not achieve what Reagan had. He did not change the political common sense. He did not move the political consensus to the left, as Reagan had moved it to the right. This failure may have more to do with his private foibles and lack of opportunity than with political factors.

Where Clinton failed as president, though, Howard Dean succeeded in his failed candidacy. As we observed in chapter 5, this was one of the remarkable achievements of the Dean campaign. Through the antiwar movement and the Dean campaign, through Internet activism, Democrats reasserted their voice. Internet activism is a very serious answer to talk radio. When it comes to assertive dogma, the left may not be an equal to the right. When it comes to serious discussion, the left may be superior.

The history of the late twentieth century was not very friendly to the grand march of the left. Between the collapse of previously existing socialism and the crises of the welfare state, the easy answers of the left came to be critically examined. And as the left turned to ideas about third ways, it also had to confront criticisms predicated on understandings that its position on capital and the limits of liberal democracy needs to be informed not only by class, but also by gender, sexual orientation, race, and a vast array of different national, ethnic, regional, and historical experiences. If anything, the discursive capacity of the left has become enriched. There is a general recognition of diverse political positions, although there still are attempts at overriding critiques of capitalism—the most ambitious is *Empire,* by Michael Hardt and Antonio Negri.[5] Contrary to the popular wisdom, the left has lost its attachment to political correctness. What was not particularly good news for the dogmatic left was very good news for a more democratic left. Feminists must now confront critical race theorists. Deconstructivists must confront postcolonial theorists. Marxists, post-Marxists, and socialists must confront the complex problems of identities and their politics. And within each of these tendencies, there is considerable debate with no official position.

Back in the 1930s, leftists could joke, with fear, about political correctness. This was the time of party lines, purges, and official truths. Now there is a field of debate. To be sure, certain central concerns, for equality and justice, against capitalism and globalization, still animate the left. But the approaches to the central concerns are varied in the extreme. These are matters to be debated, not easily agreed upon. Much of this is academic. Intellectuals debate endlessly about issues of theory and their practical consequences. And these debates are distanced from the concerns of ordinary people.[6]

When we look at the mobilization against the war and the development of electoral alternatives, the diversity of the left and its primary mode of debate over differences become apparent. Online, there is an expectation of differences of opinion, and people work on respecting the differences and finding common ground. This has been apparent in the antiwar mobilization and in electoral organizing. These are spaces for public freedom in Arendt's sense. The contrast with talk radio is stark. Internet mobilization is democratic in form, while talk radio is authoritarian. And given the history of the left and right in recent years, this means that the Internet favors the democratic left, as talk radio favors the dogmatic right.

Some cautionary notes. it is not that the Internet is inherently democratic or necessarily deliberative. It facilitates not only democratic alternatives. As we have seen in the case of the Christian right, the Internet can be supportive of undemocratic as well as democratic micropolitics. Even more seriously, it can provide a meeting ground for and validate the most reprehensible politics; the Net encourages the coming together of like-minded people without the constraints of space and so can make all sorts of marginal abominations appear normal. Interested in National Socialism and the glories of the Third Reich? Just query your favorite search engine; from there one click will take you to www.stormfront.org and an apologist's history of Nazism. Or take part in a forum for those who share racist, anti-Semitic beliefs. Learn what like-minded people think about Mel Gibson's *The Passion of the Christ,* share strategies for combating the Anti-Defamation League, or learn about upcoming white nationalist lectures and demonstrations. You are instantly part of a large movement.

The Internet makes it possible for people to gather, and much of what it supports is apolitical. Its primary subject matter is still pornography. It is increasingly being defined by commercial imperatives. And when it comes to politics, all sorts can be found. But with significant movement from the virtual to the embodied, with large-scale mobilization in response to the present state of political culture, the Internet favors a democratic politics of small things.

It is also not the case that radio is necessarily dogmatic and right-wing. It can and does provide the opportunity for in-depth reporting, refined analysis, and informed and civil discussion. National Public Radio is one of the best sources of news in the United States. Talk programs on its network are serious, civil, and informed. A broad range of views is presented. Similar programming can be found on commercial networks. It is not as if right-wing talk radio is the only political voice on the air. But this particular radio form has successfully mobilized significant rightist segments of the population. And the most promising responses from the left have been more often found on the Internet than on radio.

The Power of Definition

The medium is not the message. Rather, the politics of small things has been realized in the relation between the political contests of the time and the media platforms for the power of the powerless. Acting as if they lived in a free society, the oppositions in Central Europe presented a democratic challenge to the Soviet Empire. Through everyday interactions in university seminars, students and professors have created, or failed to create, institutions of liberal education. Through interactions among journalists, the relationship between "the media" and democracy has been changed. Through virtual interactions, people in the antiwar movement and in the Dean campaign helped redefine the politics of the day. And these alternatives to the politics of coercion are but examples used here to highlight the existence of a more general social potential that is especially important in our dark times.

Indeed, when we think of the major political leaders of the United States in the twentieth century, those who have relied on the politics of small things stand up well against more conventional political leaders. Martin Luther King Jr. stands as the archetype. The great civil rights leader had no conventional sources of political power. His power was based on a social movement of people who met, spoke to each other, and developed a capacity to act in concert. His base of power was in the politics of small things, and he, with his supporters, was as important in determining the fate of the nation as any conventional politician of the century.

When we look around the globe and at history, it is not at all clear that those who seek to oppose the powers or to resolve implacable ethnic and religious conflicts are best served by using conventional means. A strong argument can be made that the limits of hard power are as evident as the limits of soft power, and this argument is one made from the position of hard realism, not simply idealism. It has long been asserted, following Clausewitz, that war is politics by other means. The limits of this other means, given the overall distribution of coercive capacity and nuclear arms, are becoming more and more evident. The importance of the politics of small things is broadly evident.

For example, the conflict in the Middle East between Israelis and Palestinians appears to be without end. The claims of Palestinian and Israeli nationalism and self defense have led to repeated wars, with escalating terrorist and antiterrorist actions. In the Camp David talks at the end of the Clinton presidency, it appeared that the parties were on the brink of a real settlement, but failure led to an escalation of the violence and the dimming of the prospects for peace. Within this context, a group of independent Palestinians and Israelis began to meet. They negotiated an agreement among themselves on a resolution of the conflict. At a time when the official leadership on both sides claimed that they did not have a negotiating partner, and when both sides had resorted to violence and counterviolence with no positive results, two experienced official peace negotiators, the former Israeli justice minister, Yossi Beilin, and the former Palestinian information minister, Yasser Abed Rabbo, together with sympathetic colleagues, presented an alternative. They formulated an agreement on a final settlement. They revealed how a final settlement could look and won broad support from significant political actors from around the world and from a majority of Israelis and Palestinians.[7] They were denounced on both sides, but at least for a while they were able to open international discussion to address a pressing problem. While guns were fired and rocks thrown, while terrorists attacked and bombs exploded, interested people met, talked, and acted in concert, and they presented a significant alternative. In the months that followed the signing of the Geneva Accord, in December 1, 2003, its supporters continued to organize among themselves, some using Internet meet-ups. The sort of social support for a settlement that these groups were reaffirming will be necessary should peace again become a possibility.

Observing the power of such human interactions, Jonathan Schell argues that violence has become obsolete and that its political capacity has been overvalued historically.[8] He critically assesses the political capacity of violence to create fundamental change, going so far as to argue that the political changes of the French and Russian revolutions were realized without violence and that violence was only manifested in the aftermath of change. Against the backdrop of modern warfare and its links with the democratic, scientific, and industrial revolutions and with imperialism, Schell reflects on the importance of assertive nonviolent action, seeing a sort of international synthesis emerging. From the actions of Gandhi, to the work of Martin Luther King, to the democratic movement in Eastern and Central Europe, to the peaceful transitions to democracy in Spain, South Africa, and Latin America, Schell sees evidence for what he calls cooperative power. Drawing on Arendt, he maintains that the kind of political power she illuminated is the only possible way of proceeding in the nuclear age. The limits of violence have been revealed, as has the realistic potential for cooperative action. We have observed the same thing by looking closely at small things and their politics.

When ordinary people got together around the kitchen table in the former Soviet bloc, they added a new dimension to their society. Their informal interactions proved that totalitarian politics and culture have social limits, structured by ordinary people interacting with each other outside of official definition. They defined their situation as being free of political controls, and for the most part it was. The power of social definition was likewise evident as the free zone of the nontotalitarian expanded beyond such intimate settings, to the bookstore and the literary salon in Warsaw, and more spectacularly to Solidarity. The power of definition goes beyond such interactions, though, with important political implications for both the larger political stage and the struggles of everyday life. We have observed this through literary, televisual, radio, and

Internet expression. Both the way space for political expression is created and what is expressed in the space play very important political roles in our times. The power of definition is a key basis for the politics of small things. The struggle over definition is a key component of politics. This power of definition can discipline, but it also presents the possibility of redefinition through interactions among people.

Hannah Arendt closed her magnum opus, *The Origins of Totalitarianism,* on a surprisingly positive reflection: "But there remains also the truth that every end of history necessarily contains a new beginning. . . . Beginning, before it becomes a historical event, is the capacity of man; politically it is identical with man's freedom. . . . This beginning is guaranteed by each new birth; it is indeed every man."[9] Thus, her account of the rise and spread of totalitarianism concludes with an optimistic suggestion: modern barbarism may come to an end.

We have observed that the fall of one type of tyranny brings the spread of new tyrannical threats. But these threats do not stand unanswered. I have maintained that the politics of small things is part of the answer. It is the social material that makes the connection between the individual human being and the capacity to bring something new into the world. In the space that exists between people, in their interactions, they can redefine the situation and change their world in the process. This was a possibility that Arendt chose to emphasize as she closed her frightening reflections on modern tyranny and its terror. It remains a socially embedded prospect.

Postscript: 9/11 and a Friendship

I would like to close this inquiry on a personal note, to explain how this investigation has been the consequence of a friendship cut short. On September 11, 2001, I lost my dear friend Michael Asher. Mike was a new-technology genius. He lived in a different world than I. While I sat in libraries, classrooms, university seminars, and academic conferences, some I admit quite exciting, Mike jetted around the world developing software for the new economy. He worked for Canter Fitzgerald, which had its offices on the 104th floor of Tower One of the World Trade Center. He was a fast-paced person in a fast-paced world. I am more deliberate. But we found some warmly inhabited common grounds: our families, our love of hiking, and most significantly for public purposes, our curiosity about the world. This book is dedicated to the memory of Michael Edward Asher, and is inspired by his curiosity and his fate.

I began writing the manuscript before Mike's death. The attacks of

2001 changed the nature of the project. Before, it was an exploration of the political significance of the little things that went into the miraculous transformations of 1989. I wanted to understand these things and consider how general were their implications. After the attacks, it became a desperate attempt to understand how those little things might still matter. As I wrote each page, I have thought about the tragedy of my friend's end.

At times, I have been tempted to drop the project. A recurring motto of my life in recent years has been: it hurts to think. It has become easy to be pessimistic about the human prospect. Too much has become acceptable or at least commonplace, from genocide to global terror to militarized antiterror to torture in the name of antiterrorism. The capacity to address global injustices and human self-annihilation does not appear very good. When I think, things just seem worse, and I can't talk about this with my close friend. But thinking about his life and our friendship has inspired me to push on.

Much has changed since Mike's death. The democratic hopes and prosperity of the post–cold war era have been replaced by falsely perceived (to my mind) clashes of civilizations and yearnings for new authoritarian orders. Opportunities have been lost. Despair penetrates the global atmosphere. When I look at the big global actors and their interactions, I see little that is hopeful. The Europeans cogently have criticized the failings of American foreign policy, but they have not presented viable alternatives for taking responsibility for the proliferation of nuclear arms, the threat of Islamic terrorism, the appearance of genocide. The postcolonial critique of the West is telling. But is there an alternative to liberal democracy and global human rights? And would it be a good thing if there were? American-style consumerism has penetrated the consciousness of billions globally. McDonalds and Starbucks (not to be equated in my mind, given my love of good coffee) are everywhere, but criticism of this fact seems to come from cultural elites and not the broad masses of people. Ordinary people are apparently endlessly enticed by these and other goods, which promise a special version of the good life. The cultivated disdain of this choice, expressed alike by refined secular and religious intellectuals, when not willingly accepted by ordinary people, offers nothing but authoritarianism as an alternative.

Yet when people come together on their own, speak and act in each other's presence, alternatives do appear, as I have attempted to show in this investigation. As I have been making this argument, I have been trying to convince Mike. He was a practical man, skeptical of fuzzy thoughts, a man of the bottom line. But I could convince him. When I argued that in the former Soviet bloc, it was in the end the idealists who dared to speak truth to power, to constitute the power of the powerless, who were the realists, Mike was convinced, even before the fateful transformations of 1989. The so-called idealists understood the nature of the totalitarian house of cards and acted practically. The realists who accepted the order of things proved to be fools. And it is my hope that Mike would have understood the extension of that argument to our present circumstance.

The politics of small things has and will make a difference, in everyday life, in political contests such as the American election, and in the global arena. There are alternatives, and recognizing them and acting upon them is not naïve idealism but solid, sociologically grounded realism.

Notes

INTRODUCTION

1. Key guides for discerning the meaning of the twentieth century are Hannah Arendt, Eric Hobsbawm, and François Furet. See Arendt, *The Origins of Totalitarianism* (New York: Harcourt Brace Jovanovich, 1973), Furet, *The Passing of an Illusion: The Idea of Communism in the Twentieth Century* (Chicago: University of Chicago Press, 2000), and Hobsbawm, *Age of Extremes: A History of the World, 1914–1991* (New York: Random House, 1996).

2. See Jeffrey C. Goldfarb, *After the Fall: The Pursuit of Democracy in Central Europe* (New York: Basic Books, 1992).

3. This is the position of the Nobel laureate Milton Friedman, for example. For his general position on the state and the economy see Friedman, *Why Government Is the Problem* (Stanford: Hoover Institution Press, 1993).

4. See Joseph Stiglitz, *Globalization and Its Discontents* (New York: W. W. Norton, 2003), for the position of a competing Nobel laureate.

5. See Milan Kundera, *The Unbearable Lightness of Being* (New York: Harper Collins, 1999), for an imaginative critical account of the grand march.

6. See Edward S. Herman and Noam Chomsky, *Manufacturing Consent: The Political Economy of the Mass Media* (New York: Pantheon, 2002).

7. Bernard Goldberg, *Bias: A CBS Insider Exposes How the Media Distort the News* (Washington, D.C.: Regnery Publications, 2002).

8. Thomas first explored the implications of the problem of the definition of the situation in his study of the social psychol-

ogy of young women. See W. I. Thomas, *The Unadjusted Girl* (Boston: Little Brown, 1923).

CHAPTER ONE

1. See Jeffrey C. Goldfarb, "Why Is There No Feminism after Communism?" *Social Research,* vol. 64, no. 2, Summer 1997.

2. Goldfarb, *After the Fall.*

3. As Stalin did in the show trials of the 30s. See Kundera, *Unbearable Lightness of Being,* for an intriguing fictive exploration of this.

4. Michel Foucault, "Truth and Power," in *The Foucault Reader,* ed. Paul Rabinow (New York: Pantheon, 1984), 74–75.

5. Arendt, *Origins of Totalitarianism,* 307.

6. Hannah Arendt, "Truth and Politics," in *Between Past and Future* (New York: Penguin Books, 1977), 256.

7. Max Horkheimer and Theodor Adorno, *Dialectic of Enlightenment* (New York: Continuum, 1990).

8. Richard Sennett, *The Fall of Public Man* (New York: W. W. Norton, 1992).

9. Hannah Arendt, "What Is Freedom?" in *Between Past and Future,* 154–55.

10. Ibid., 156–65.

11. See Hannah Arendt, *The Human Condition,* ed. Robert Cummings, forward by Peter L. Berger (Albany: State University of New York Press, 2001), 38–50.

12. Arendt, *Origins of Totalitarianism,* 250–66.

13. This is how she concludes *The Origins of Totalitarianism.* It is highlighted in her key chapter "Ideology and Terror."

14. Jeffrey C. Goldfarb, *Civility and Subversion: The Intellectual in Democratic Society* (Cambridge: Cambridge University Press, 1998).

15. I have reservations about this common observation, because I believe that the term *ideology* has a more specific meaning than such an assertion assumes. See my *Civility and Subversion,* 13–16.

CHAPTER TWO

1. The description of the events of 1968 that follows is drawn from my research on Polish theater, first reported in Jeffrey C. Goldfarb, *The Persistence of Freedom: The Sociological Implications of Polish Student Theater* (Boulder: Westview, 1980).

2. These theaters were originally part of the new socialist order, supported by the new authorities, in the immediate aftermath of World War II. They were quite similar to amateur theater groups in American communities. They took on a political role during the Stalinist era, producing agit-prop theater throughout the People's Poland. They then became one of the first forums for criticizing the Stalinist order and from the fall of the Stalinists in 1956 through the fall of the communist regime, a vibrant part of the critical cultural world. The history of this theater is presented in my *Persistence of Freedom.*

3. See Susan E. Reid and David Crowley, eds., *Style and Socialism: Modernity and Material Culture in Post-War Eastern Europe* (New York: Berg, 2000).

4. Vaclav Havel, "The Power of the Powerless," in *Open Letters: Selected Writings, 1965–1990,* ed. Paul Wilson (New York: Vintage, 1992).

5. Erving Goffman, *Interaction Rituals: Essays on Face-to-Face Behavior* (London: Allan Lane, 1972).

6. Erving Goffman, *The Presentation of Self in Everyday Life* (New York: Overlook Press, 1973).

7. Goffman, *Interaction Rituals.*

8. Erving Goffman, *Frame Analysis: An Essay on the Organization of Experience* (Boston: Northeastern University Press, 1986).

9. Erving Goffman, *Asylums: Essays on the Social Situation of Mental Patients and Other Inmates* (New York: Anchor Books, 1961).

10. Goffman, *Frame Analysis,* 1–2.

11. Adam Michnik, "The New Evolutionism," in *Letters from Prison and Other Essays* (Berkeley: University of California Press, 1987).

CHAPTER THREE

1. The following account is drawn from reports published in the *New York Times* — see Bernard Gwertzman and Michael Kaufman, eds., *The Collapse of Communism* (New York: Times Books, 1990)—supplemented by the analysis presented in Andrei Codrescu, *The Hole in the Flag* (New York: William Morrow, 1991), Vladimir Tismaneanu, *Fantasies of Salvation: Democracy, Nationalism, and Myth in Post-Communist Europe* (Princeton: Princeton University Press, 1998), Vladimir Tismaneanu, "The First Post-Communist Decade," *Romanian Journal of Society and Politics* 1, no. 1 (summer 2001): 5–15, and Vladimir Tismaneanu and Gail Kligman, "Romania's First Post-Communist Decade: From Iliescu to Iliescu," *East European Constitutional Review* 10, no. 1 (winter 2000): 78–83.

2. See chapter 8 for a discussion of the limits of the significance of television in the changes in Romania then, as compared to the politics of television now.

3. This account draws upon reports in the *New York Times* (see Gwertzman and Kaufman, *Collapse of Communism),* and upon the analysis of Timothy Garton Ash in his *The Magic Lantern: The Revolution of '89 Witnessed in Warsaw, Budapest and Prague* (New York: Random House, 1990).

4. See Havel, "Power of the Powerless."

5. See Michnik, "New Evolutionism."

6. For a cogent analysis of the roundtable as a new political invention see Ralitsa Peeva, "The Bulgarian Round Table in Comparative Perspective" (PhD diss., New School, Graduate Faculty, Department of Sociology, 2001).

7. I present a critique of the civil society position in my *Civility and Subversion.*

8. Goldfarb, *Civility and Subversion.*

CHAPTER FOUR

1. See Hobsbawm, *Age of Extremes*. This periodization is admittedly a Western one, centered on the experiences of Europe and North America. Nonetheless, given the North Atlantic hegemony of the globe in the past centuries, it applies to much that goes beyond this sphere.

2. For telling analyses of the politics of religion, and especially its contribution for democratic publics, see José Casanova, *Public Religions in the Modern World* (Chicago: University of Chicago Press, 1994), and Talal Asad, *Genealogies of Religion: Discipline and Reasons of Power in Christianity and Islam* (Baltimore: Johns Hopkins University Press, 1993).

3. George W. Bush, "Remarks by the President at the Islamic Center of Washington, D.C.," September 17, 2001, http://www.whitehouse.gov./news/releases/2001/09/print/20010917-11.html.

4. Steven Erlanger, "Italy's Premier Calls Western Civilization Superior to Islamic World," *New York Times*, September 27, 2001, A8.

5. Salman Rushdie, "Yes, This Is About Islam," *New York Times*, November 2, 2001, A26.

6. Christopher Hitchens, "Minority Report," *Nation*, October 8, 2001.

7. This bin Laden quote is drawn from an excerpted transcript in the *New York Times*, December 14, 2001. The video was recorded on November 9, 2001, and made available by American authorities on December 13, 2001.

8. Peter L. Bergen, *Holy War, Inc.: Inside the Secret World of Osama bin Laden* (New York: Free Press, 2001), 19. The quote is from an interview Bergen conducted for a CNN documentary.

9. Ibid., 20–21.

10. Excerpted from transcript of November 9, 2001, Bin Laden video, *New York Times*, December 14, 2001.

11. Bergen, *Holy War, Inc.*, 34. The quote is from an interview with Musharaf by Arnaud de Borchgrave, *Washington Times*, March 21, 2000.

12. See my "How to Be an Intelligent Anti-American," *Logos* 1, no. 1 (winter 2002): 14–27.

13. Arendt, "What Is Authority?" in *Between Past and Future*, 99–100. See also her *Origins of Totalitarianism*, 364–88.

14. Bergen, *Holy War, Inc.*, 29.

15. For a comparison of Islamic public life with the public life of the Enlightenment, see Talal Asad, "Religious Criticism in the Middle East: Notes on Islamic Public argument," in his *Genealogies of Religion*, 200–238.

16. Bergen, *Holy War, Inc.*, 23.

17. Ibid., 26.

18. Reported in John F. Burns, "Purchasing Power: When Seeing Osama Is Not Enough," *New York Times*, Sunday, January 6, 2002, sec. 4, p. 16.

19. Bernard Lewis, *What Went Wrong? The Clash Between Islam and Modernity in the Middle East* (New York: Perennial City, 2003).

20. See Talal Asad, "Europe against Islam: Islam in Europe," *Muslim World* 87, no. 2 (April 1997): 183–95, and José Casanova, "Civil Society and Religion: Retrospective Reflections on Catholicism and Prospective Reflections on Islam," *Social Research* 69, no. 4 (winter 2002): 1041–80.

21. George W. Bush, "Address to a Joint Session of Congress and the American People," September 20, 2001, http://whitehouse.gov/news/releases/2001/09/print/20010920-8.html.

22. He carefully did not condemn communism as a defeated enemy in hopes of enlisting the support of China in the war against terrorism.

23. George W. Bush, "Statement by the President in His Address to the Nation," September 11, 2001, http://www.whitehouse.gov/news/releases/2001/09/print/20010911-16.html.

24. "Full text of Tony Blair's Speech, made today from Downing Street," September 12, 2001, http://www.guardian.co.uk/wtccrash/story/0,1300,550655,00.html.

25. Bush, "Address to Joint Session."

26. George W. Bush, "President's Remarks at National Day of Prayer and Remembrance, The National Cathedral, Washington, D.C.," http://www.whitehouse.gov/news/releases/2001/09/print/20010914-2.html.

27. Bush briefly used the loaded term, but quickly abandoned it when its inflammatory connotations in the Islamic world brought immediate negative reaction.

28. Michael Walzer, "First, Define the Battlefield," *New York Times,* September 21, 2001, A35.

29. William Kristol, "Bush vs. Powell," *Washington Post,* September 25, 2001, A23.

30. See William Kristol, "The Wrong Strategy," *Washington Post,* October 30, 2001, and, in the *Weekly Standard,* Robert Kagan and William Kristol, "A War to Win," September 24, 2001, 7, "The Right War," October 1, 2001, 9, and "Fighting to Win," November 12, 2001, 9.

31. Mark Gevisser, "Dispatches: South Africa," *Nation,* October 15, 2001, 5.

32. Noam Chomsky, "On the Bombing," *Al-Ahram Weekly Online,* no. 552, September 20–26, 2001.

33. Arundhati Roy, "The Algebra of Infinite Justice," *Guardian Unlimited,* September 29, 2001, ttp://www.guardian.co.uk/Saturday_review/story/0,3605,559756,00.html.

34. Arundhati Roy, "Brutality Smeared in Peanut Butter: Why America Must Stop the War Now," *Guardian Unlimited,* October 23, 2001, http://www.guardian.co.uk/g2/story/0,,579191,00.html.

35. See Furet, *Passing of an Illusion.*

36. Richard Bernstein, "Counterpoint to Unity: Dissent," *New York Times,* October 6, 2001, A14.

37. Dennis Brown, "US Critics under Fire," *Guardian,* October 1, 2001, http://www.guardian.co.uk/letters/story/0,,560945,00.html.

38. Arundhati Roy, *The God of Small Things* (New York: Random House, 1997), 73.

39. Ibid., 320.

40. Milan Kundera, *The Art of the Novel* (New York: Grove Press, 1988).

CHAPTER FIVE

1. Andrew Boyd, "The Web Wires the Movement," *Nation,* August 4, 2003, 13–14. The descriptions of the international protests were drawn from this piece.

2. Quoted in ibid.

3. Gary Wolf, "How the Internet Invented Howard Dean," *Wired,* December 24, 2003, http://www.wired.com/wired/archive/12-01/dean.html. The description of the connection between MoveOn, Meetup.com, and the Dean campaign is drawn from this article.

4. Quoted from a "rush transcript" posted at http://transcripts.cnn.com/TRANSCRIPTS/0401/09/pzn.00.html. The quotes that follow come from a news alert sent out by the Dean Rapid Response Network on January 10, 2004.

5. Daniel Okrent, "Dr. Dean Assumes His Place on the Examining Table," *New York Times* Week in Review, January 18, 2004, 2.

6. Dean Rapid Response Network news alert, January 10, 2004.

7. Jim Rutenberg, "A Concession Rattles the Rafters (and Some Dean Supporters)," *New York Times,* January 21, 2004, A24.

8. Siegel made the comment during his discussion with Bill Powers, media critic for the *National Journal. All Things Considered,* National Public Radio, January 21, 2004

9. Rutenberg, "Concession Rattles the Rafters."

10. McKenzie Wark, *Virtual Geography: Living with Global Media Events* (Bloomington: Indiana University Press, 1994).

11. Reported in Amy Harmon, "Politics of the Web: Meet, Greet, Segregate, Meet Again," *New York Times,* Week in Review, January 25, 2004, 16.

12. Jurgen Habermas, *The Structural Transformation of the Public Sphere: An Inquiry into a Category of Bourgeois Society* (Cambridge: MIT Press, 1989).

13. Maureen Dowd, "Squished Cupcakes and Polls," *New York Times,* Week In Review, January 25, 2004, 15.

14. Samuel Pratt, "Dowd does it again," e-mail correspondence on Dean Rapid Response Network, January 25, 2004.

15. Andres Martinez, "Will We Remember 2004 as the Year of the Dean Bubble?" *New York Times,* January 30, 2004, A24.

16. For a preliminary account, see Glenn Justice and Jodi Wilgoren, "Figures Detail Dean's Slide From Solvent to Struggling," *New York Times,* February 2, 2004, A18.

17. Joshua Meyrowitz, *No Sense of Place: The Impact of Electronic Media on Social Behavior* (Oxford: Oxford University Press, 1985).

18. I think that the system of measurement could not discern who in fact had the larger vote in Florida, and that luck, persistence, and an unsteady Supreme Court combined to give George W. Bush the presidency.

19. See Paul Krugman, *The Great Unraveling: Losing Our Way in the New Century* (New York: W. W. Norton, 2003).

20. Jeffrey C. Goldfarb, *The Cynical Society: The Culture of Politics and the Politics of Culture in American Life* (Chicago: University of Chicago Press, 1991).

CHAPTER SIX

1. See Louis Menand, "Permanent Fatal Errors: Did the Voters Send a Message?" *New Yorker,* December 6, 2004, 54–60, for an interesting report of a meeting of political scientists and pollsters at Stanford University to analyze polling results a week after the elections.

2. Richard A. Viguerie and David Franke, *America's Right Turn: How Conservatives Used New and Alternative Media to Take Power* (Chicago: Bonus Books, 2004).

3. For a report on this comparison see, Julia Duin, "Christian Youths Targeted for Votes," *Washington Times,* August 12, 2004, A01.

4. The quotes from the Christian Coalition are taken from its Web site, as it appeared on December 20, 2004, http://www.cc.org/getinvolved.cfm.

5. Kimberly Conger, "Evangelicals: Outside the Beltway," in "Religion and the 2004 Election," special supplement, *Religion in the News,* fall 2003, http://www.trincoll.edu/depts/csrpl/RINVol6No3/2004%20Election/outside%20 beltway%20evangelicals.htm.

6. For a careful analysis of the political activity of clergy see, James Guth, Linad Beail, Greg Crow, Beverly Graddy, Steve Montreal, Brent Nelsen, James Penning, and Jeff Walz, "The Political Activity of Evangelical Clergy in the Election of 2000: A Case Study of Five Denominations," *Journal of the Scientific Study of Religion* 42, no. 4 (2003): 501–14.

7. Wayne Slater, "Bush Campaign Reaches Out to 'Friendly Congregations' in Battleground States," TheState.com, October 19, 2004.

8. See Gordon Wood, *The Radicalism of the American Revolution* (New York: Knopf, 1992).

9. Alan Cooperman, "Evangelical Leaders Appeal to Followers to Go to the Polls," *Washington Post,* October 15, 2004, A6.

10. Rev. Jerry Johnston of First Family Church, Overland Park, Kansas, quoted in Brad Cooper, "'Pastor Briefings' to Focus on Political Involvement," KansasCity.com, September 21, 2004.

11. "In the South: Church Notes," *Religion in the News* 6, no. 1 (spring 2003).

12. Nathan Burchfiel, "Christian Group Wants Politics at the Pulpit," CNSnews.com, July 27, 2004.

13. See Ted Olsen, comp., "Weblog: Bush Campaign Seeks 'Friendly Congregations,'" ChristianityToday.com, June 3, 2004, http://www.christianitytoday .com/ct/2004/122/42.0.html.

14. This is a central idea in my depiction of the democratic role of intellectuals; see my *Civility and Subversion.*

15. See Alexis de Tocqueville, *Democracy in America,* vol. 2, bk. 1.

CHAPTER SEVEN

1. See Elzbieta Matynia, *Grappling with Democracy: Deliberations on Post Communist Societies, 1990–1995* (Prague: Sociologicke Nakladastvi, 1996), for an account of this seminar and some documentation of its work, and for an account of its connection with later collaborations.

2. Hannah Arendt, "Crisis in Education," in *Between Past and Future,* 177.

3. Michael Oakeshott, *The Voice of Liberal Learning* (New Haven: Yale University Press, 1989), 63.

4. Ibid., 41.

5. Liberalism, as a political doctrine and type of political regime, and liberal education are different. Although liberal political orders are relatively friendly places for liberal education (i.e., states that are formally restricted in their interventions in cultural life tend to leave liberal arts educational institutions alone), liberal education is not only constituted in this negative fashion. It is a positive cultural endeavor, where the educational transaction between generations is linked to the question of what it means to be human. But it is a problematic cultural endeavor. On the problematic relationship between liberal orders and cultural freedom, see my *On Cultural Freedom: An Exploration of Public Life in Poland and America* (Chicago: University of Chicago Press, 1982).

6. See discussion in the introduction.

7. See, for example, E. J. Dionne Jr., *Why Americans Hate Politics* (New York: Simon and Schuster, 1991), and Christopher Lasch, "Journalism, Publicity, and the Lost Art of Argument," *Gannet Center Journal,* 4, no. 2 (1990): 1–11.

8. See James M. Fallows, *Breaking the News: How the Media Undermine American Democracy* (New York: Knopf, 1996).

9. Davis Merritt, "Democracy from the Bottom Up," *Wichita Eagle,* October 27, 1996.

10. See Chris Conte, "Civic Journalism," *Congressional Quarterly Governing,* August 1996, 819–37, http://governing.com/archive/1996/Aug/Press.txt.

11. For a highly critical overview see Michael Kelly, "Media Culpa," *New Yorker,* November 4, 1996, 45–49.

12. These examples are taken from Conte, "Civic Journalism."

13. See Max Frankel, "Fix-It Journalism," *New York Times Magazine,* May 21, 1995, pp. 28, 30.

14. The *New York Times* series "How Race is Lived in America" ran June 4–July 16, 2000, with a total of fifteen articles. "Portraits of Grief" ran September 14, 2001–February 2, 2002, and was later supplemented by about four hundred additional portraits. Both series won Pulitzer Prizes.

CHAPTER EIGHT

1. Wark, Virtual Geography.

2. Bergen, *Holy War, Inc.*

3. Arendt, "Truth and Politics" and "What Is Freedom?"

4. Daniel Boorstein, *The Image: A Guide to Pseudo-Events in America* (New York: Vintage, 1992). Neil Postman, *Amusing Ourselves to Death: Public Discourse in the Age of Show Business* (New York: Penguin, 1986).

5. Michael Schudson, *Good Citizen: A History of American Civic Life* (Cambridge: Harvard University Press, 1999).

6. Kenneth Cmiel, *Democratic Eloquence: The Fight over Popular Speech*

in Nineteenth-Century America (Berkeley: University of California Press, 1991).

7. Bruce Ackerman, *We the People,* 2 vols. (Cambridge: Harvard University Press, 1993).

8. Garry Wills, *Inventing America: Jefferson's Declaration of Independence* (New York: Vintage, 1979).

9. Alex Williams, "Live From Miami," *New York Times,* September 26, 2004, sec. 9, p. 1. William O'Rourke, *Chicago Sun-Times* Sunday edition, September 26, 2004, 39. David Warren, Editorial/Opinion, *Windsor Star,* September 18, 2004, A6.

10. Kathleen Hall Jamieson, *Eloquence in an Electronic Age: The Transformation of Political Speechmaking* (New York: Oxford University Press, 1990).

11. He made these observations in a public presentation at the sociology department of the New School for Social Research in 1999.

12. The Trippi blog can be found at http://changeforamerica.com/blog.

13. Arendt, "Truth and Politics," 263.

14. Arendt, *Human Condition,* 198.

15. Joshua Meyrowitz, *No Sense of Place: The Impact of Electronic Media on Social Behavior* (Oxford: Oxford University Press, 1985).

16. On the Lewinsky scandal, see Martin Plot, "Deliberative Scenes and Democratic Politics in the Lewinsky Case," *Constellations* 6, no. 2 (June 1999): 167–76.

CONCLUSION

1. Goldfarb, *Cynical Society.*

2. Viguerie and Franke, *America's Right Turn.*

3. Sheldon Drobny, *Road to Air America: Breaking the Right Wing Stranglehold on Our Nation's Airwaves* (New York: Select Books, 2004). Jesse Walker, *Rebels on the Air: An Alternative History of Radio in America* (New York: New York University Press, 2001). David Barker, *Rushed to Judgment: Talk Radio and American Political Behavior* (New York: Columbia University Press, 2002).

4. For a report on the fate of this venture in liberal talk radio, see Jacques Steinberg, "Office Politics Give Liberal Talk Radio a Rocky Road," *New York Times,* May 31, 2004, C1, C6.

5. Michael Hardt and Antonio Negri, *Empire* (Cambridge: Harvard University Press, 2000).

6. Richard Rorty, *Achieving Our Country: Leftist Thought in Twentieth-Century America* (Cambridge: Harvard University Press, 1999).

7. Among the supporters were "fifty-eight former presidents, prime ministers, foreign ministers and other global leaders, among them former presidents Mikhail Gorbachev of the Soviet Union and F. W. de Klerk of South Africa, [who] issued a statement expressing 'strong support' for the plan. Other world leaders who voiced their backing included King Hassan III of Morocco, British Prime Minister Tony Blair, President Hosni Mubarak of Egypt and Clinton."

See http://www.haaretz.com/hasen/pages/ShArt.jhtml?itemNo=349832. A poll published soon after suggested that 55.6 percent of Palestinians and 53 percent of Israelis backed the principles of the Geneva Accord. See http://news.bbc.co.uk/1/hi/world/middle_east/3245838.stm.

8. Jonathan Schell, *The Unconquerable World* (New York: Metropolitan Books, 2003).

9. Arendt, *Origins of Totalitarianism,* 478–79.

Index